D1332410

Bad Company

BAD COMPANY

A WOMAN FACE TO FACE WITH THE TALIBAN

*The true story of the first female soldier
to engage in combat and kill a Taliban fighter at
close quarters.*

Chantelle Taylor

BAD COMPANY

The right of Chantelle Taylor to be identified as the Author of the Work has been asserted by her in accordance with the Copyright, Designs and Patents Act 1988

Copyright © 2011 Chantelle Taylor
First published in Great Britain in 2011 by DRA Publishing (publishers)
Publication Rights © DRA Publishing

All rights reserved. Apart from any use permitted under UK copyright law no part of this publication may be reproduced, stored in a retrieval system, or transmitted, in any form or by any means without the prior written permission of the publisher, nor be otherwise circulated in any form of binding or cover other than that in which it is published and without a similar condition being imposed on the subsequent purchaser.

No part of this work can be copied, loaned or sold to a third party in respect of editorial, film or drama script without legal authorisation from the publisher, that being DRA Publishing.

A CIP catalogue record for this title is available from the British Library
ISBN 978 0955 7813 22
Typeset: Book Antiqua
Printed and bound by Fourway Printers Ltd

Howeson Court, 14 Mary Seacole Road,
The Millfields, Plymouth PL1 3JY

BAD COMPANY

A WOMAN FACE TO FACE WITH THE TALIBAN

This book is dedicated to B Company.
The Argyll and Sutherland Highlanders
5 SCOTS

Chantelle Taylor

BAD COMPANY

The following account is based on experience serving as lead medic to B Company of 5 Scots. The Author has made her best endeavour to report events accurately and truthfully, and any insult or injury to any of the parties described or quoted herein or to their families is unintentional. The publisher is prepared to make any necessary changes in future editions.

THE MAN IN THE ARENA

"It is not the critic who counts; not the man who points out how the strong man stumbles, or where the doer of deeds could have done them better. The credit belongs to the man who is actually in the arena, whose face is marred by dust and sweat and blood; who strives valiantly; who errs, who comes short again and again, because there is no effort without error and shortcoming; but who does actually strive to do the deeds; who knows great enthusiasms, the great devotions; who spends himself in a worthy cause; who at the best knows in the end the triumph of high achievement, and who at the worst, if he fails, at least fails while daring greatly, so that his place shall never be with those cold and timid souls who neither know victory nor defeat."

Theodore Roosevelt

Carried by my Grandfather when he served in Korea with 41 Commando RM. It gave him inspiration.

PROLOGUE

The first explosion rocked the vehicle, smashing my head against the front of the wagon. I could hear rounds zipping through the antennas above me. 'What the fuck?' I shouted as an array of munitions continued to rain down.

I was travelling in the same vehicle as Kev Coyle, the OC's signaller, a tough Scotsman who was fiercely proud of his regiment, The Argyll and Sutherland Highlanders. The lightly armoured convoy in which I was travelling had turned into a Taliban shooting gallery; the noise was deafening from incoming fire from left and rear. Our heavy machine guns roared into action as broken brick and clouds of dust enveloped us.

Our Land Rover was the second vehicle in the packet, and was taking sustained and heavy fire. Looking up through the hatch I could see rounds pinging from left to right, apparently from enemy on my side of the vehicle. I heard someone shout, 'Get some fucking rounds down!' Popping back up for a split second, I got eyes on the insurgent who was engaging us, 30 metres away and to the half right of me.

Suddenly overwhelmed by a fear that I was about to be shot in the face, I experienced a massive rush of blood to the head and took in a mouthful of dust as I reminded myself to breathe. Instinctively and purposefully, I engaged him.

The excitement that I felt before moving into Marjah was fading fast. Kev, covering our right side, engaged another fighter close by. The Minimi gunner in the vehicle behind us took on two insurgents who had positioned themselves on the roof of a compound.

Shouting out half of a fire control order, I alerted my team to targets around us. Just then a lull in the firefight was filled with the sound of the dreaded cry 'Man Down! Man Down!' blasting across the radio net. As I scanned for further threats, Major Harry Clark, our OC, shouted through to the back of our rover. 'One times casualty in the rear vehicle, Sgt T!'

He calmly jumped out of the front seat as I climbed through the back door to meet him. We started to run to the back of the convoy, all the while aware that we were both vulnerable to enemy fire. Despite the baking Afghan sun, the med pack on my back feeling like it was housing a fridge freezer, we made light work of the distance on foot that we covered. Midway there, however, the OC stopped and turned back towards our vehicle.

I didn't ask why, I just followed him; it wasn't out of lack of interest, my lungs needed oxygen more than I needed a conversation. I jumped back into the wagon and struggled to breathe. Kev laughed. 'You all right mucker?'

I wanted to share the joke that I was in and out of our vehicle like a fucking yo-yo, but I was 'physically hanging out'- exhausted. Our vehicle shunted forward and we hastily moved off. Back on top cover, I was desperate to cool down and wanted to take my helmet off but couldn't. Slowly I recomposed myself, Kev still laughing at my ordeal of running in the midday heat.

Reaching an open area, the OC sent our snipers up to a compound roof to take out any potential threats. The Apache or UGLY callsign was now on station and along with our snipers was hunting the Taliban of Marjah. Chuckie had taken a round to the abdomen; having assessed him quickly, I left him in the capable hands of LCpl Tom Rooke while I briefed the OC on his condition. His wound was high and I was inclined to think that he might develop a chest injury, so his evacuation needed to be swift.

Casualty extraction under fire wasn't without risk; the inbound Chinook was escorted by two Apaches, which circled our position like birds of prey before the Chinook swept in.

Chuckie was airborne within 30 minutes of being hit. Reassured, I sorted out my kit out before mounting up again with the rest of B Company.

This was my first taste of close quarter combat; little did I know that B Company would be under fire almost every day for the next two months. In Bad Company, I tell the story of a band of brothers under siege: the men of B Company 5 SCOTS, The Argyll and Sutherland Highlanders.

CHAPTER ONE

Game On

I knew that getting their attention would not be easy. This is the first of a whole series of lectures they will attend this week. It's early 2008 and I had been selected to oversee the haemorrhage control training for 16 Air Assault Brigade prior to the unit's deployment on Operation Herrick 8, the Ministry of Defence's title for the British Forces operating in Afghanistan. My team had travelled in the early hours of this morning from our base at Colchester in Essex to Rock barracks in Suffolk, the home of 23 Engineer Regiment (Air Assault). A cross-section of Officers, Sergeants and private soldiers stand around waiting for my brief. I run through it one final time in my head. The more senior among them would have heard similar briefs before. Lectures can be boring, so mine had to be delivered in a manner that these soldiers would remember. If they didn't then I was wasting my time and theirs. Haemorrhage control, in laymans' terms is making sure that guys on the ground know how to stop bleeding. The fighting in Helmand is violent and injuries are often catastrophic.

Early application of a tourniquet is paramount. A soldier will bleed to death from a serious wound very quickly if life-saving interventions are delayed. All soldiers heading for Helmand know that the threat of serious injury is high.

Like so many military campaigns the intensity of the fighting in southern Afghanistan has forced the military medical profession to raise its game and develop new procedures in dealing with trauma. Since British troops first went into southern Afghanistan in 2006, the standard of care has soared to a level that has seen change across the medical profession the world over. We have seen new methods employed to stop bleeding, to deal with burns and save limbs.

Today, it is my job to make sure they know how to use the medical equipment that they are issued with. Basic procedures must become as instinctive to them as the drills that they carry out on their personal weapon systems. Quickly scanning the group to my front I introduce myself to them and explain what they are going to be learning about and why it is so important. Raising my voice slightly I fire straight into the brief with the well rehearsed words I have used many times. 'Don't wait until the dressing is completely piss wrapped before you decide to apply a tourniquet'. I wanted my words to be at the forefront of their minds.

Remember, 'Piss - wrapped', 'Apply' and 'Tourniquet'. You might not have heard 'piss wrapped' if you are not in the military. It's a very basic expression to describe a bandage soaked through and dripping with blood. If they didn't take anything else away from today then I wanted them to be able to apply a tourniquet as a drill and not as a last resort. Last resort in my world means potentially unsalvageable.

As the words rolled off my tongue I noticed a very familiar face standing among the group. I rattled my brain desperate to identify this elusive character. Some members of the group smirked every time that I used an expletive or an adjective of a less then polite nature. Maybe the fact that he was the last person that I expected to be standing in the group had somehow allowed me to forget one of the most famous faces on the planet.

I dragged my mind back to the importance of early tourniquet application, describing situations where more could and should have been done to save life or limb. I cited the needless death of ten-year-old Nigerian boy Damilola Taylor, who died after being stabbed in the leg with a broken bottle. A 100 metre trail of blood showed where Damilola had managed to crawl to his home in Peckham in London. The injury severed his femoral artery, causing severe blood loss.

Bystanders at the scene tried to stem the flow of blood but Damilola was certified dead on arrival to hospital. This was a classic case of a situation in which the simple application of an improvised tourniquet may have helped, although clearly he had terribly injuries.

The group listened intently, they all knew the importance of what was being said, if they were to stand any chance of surviving if they were hit by an IED blast in Helmand Province. Most lifesaving is done at the point of wounding and how soldiers deal with themselves or their comrades usually dictates the outcome of our wounded. It didn't take long before I noticed my own Squadron Sergeant Major 'H' Harris at the back of the group chuckling to himself.

Suddenly the penny dropped and I realised who the familiar face in the group was. The Sgt Major would later joke about that moment. I had spent two years at a training depot where I had been used to the direct approach with new recruits. I had never been one to hold back when it came to communication. It's all too easy to be tempted to dress things up, make ourselves sound more important than we actually are, but the harsh reality is that blokes just want to hear it how it is, they don't want spin. They certainly don't need to be patronised with the sometimes irritating over use of big words.

As the brief finishes my now very familiar guest approaches me and I don't know whether to salute him or curtsy. I could feel the burn of my now reddening cheeks, embarrassed for not realising who he was. Pausing for a moment I brace up quickly taking hold of his outstretched hand I introduce myself to Prince William, the future King of England.

'Hi Sir, how is it going?' I say loudly trying to deflect the fact that I hadn't recognised him. The Prince, accompanied by another officer smiles as he replies, 'Thanks for that Sgt Taylor it was very informative'. My eyes are still on my Sgt Major who is taking great delight in the fact that I am completely uncomfortable in the situation that is far removed from my control.

The future head of our armed forces continues to discuss the hazards that accompany the applications of tourniquets, dressings and Quick Clot which is a granular form of haemorrhage control. This is generally used when a tourniquet is deemed inappropriate, places such as the groin, artery crossovers and arm pits, more recently developed as gauze.

Wounds can be patched with minimal damage to surrounding tissue. Much of these new techniques were introduced as a direct result of US Special Forces Operations in Mogadishu, made famous through the film 'Black Hawk Down'.

I explain that these products are very good and have saved lives, but in extreme situations can cause serious complications to the patient. I add 'When all is said and done Sir, our main effort on the ground is to plug the holes and give the surgeons at the hospital in Camp Bastion a fighting chance of saving our injured and we do this by any means possible. '

As I finish my thorough almost robotic explanation of the ups and downs of such treatments, Prince William smiles and seems to approve of my final statement, nodding his head in agreement. I brace up once more as he thanks me again before moving off to his next briefing. While the Prince has never deployed to Helmand as part of a fighting unit, he has made significant visits to both Kandahar and Camp Bastion, ultimately boosting morale of the troops on the ground.

Making good the kit and equipment strewn about the place I see my next group. I take a moment to think about the situation and briefing Prince William. Much had changed for me, the girl who had left a council estate 11 years earlier. I am Sgt Chantelle Taylor, a 32 year old Combat Medical Technician, serving in support of the British Army's 16 Air Assault Brigade. A force of paratroopers, air assault infantry soldiers and a host of specialist units from engineers to medics who go to war by helicopter, transport plane and parachute.

Enlisting as a Private soldier in April 1998, I experienced active service in Kosovo, Sierra Leone, Iraq and Afghanistan I often think that this life less ordinary offered me the direction that I often lacked growing up. I was able to undertake further education and rose through the ranks

I had been selected for promotion and recommended for a Commission, which would have resulted in me becoming an officer. My development as a soldier peaked during my final tour of Helmand. It was here that I was able to apply all of the skills which I had acquired during the countless number of exercises, operations and arduous courses that came before it. I served in support of the infantry many of whom were part of our so called 'Playstation generation'.

My experience in southern Afghanistan was a combination of deliberate violence, hilarious episodes of human nature and moments of heroic madness. I am lead medic attached to B Company of (5 SCOTS), The Argyll and Sutherland Highlanders. We are well into our tour of Helmand Province when we are tasked to patrol into a place called Nad-e Ali, which is north of our main operating base in Laskhar Gah.

Our convoy moves cautiously across the desert. We hear the thud of several explosions ahead the noise carried on the dry air, who knows what is happening.

We have left our base in Lashkar Gah and are heading north west. In total we are a force of just 62 troops drawn from two Platoons and are travelling in ten heavily armed vehicles. Many of our soldiers are very young and this is their first tour in Afghanistan. In this unbearable heat they are pumped up in uncomfortable body armour and helmets, scanning the desert for anything that could pose a threat. The Company has been tasked with what is called a 'look see' patrol out to Nad-e Ali, 15 km north west of Lashkar Gah.

Our mission has come about as a direct result of a spiked increase, in enemy activity. There had been rumours that a company from one of The Parachute Regiment battalions would be committed to the area, but they are already assigned to a major operation which the Brigade had been planning for some time and would consume much of their manpower.

It involved delivering a 300 tonne turbine by convoy from Kandahar across open desert to the hydro-electric dam at Kajaki. The dam was built with funding from US Aid, an American development charity in 1975, but only two turbines were delivered before the Soviets invaded in 1979. Work stalled and the dam was unable to fully function. In 2006, when the first British troops arrived, one of the first projects identified to help the community was a project to complete the work at the dam.

In 2008, 16 Brigade had the responsibility of getting a huge convoy carrying the third turbine and additional mechanical items to the dam which it was hoped would allow contractors to commission the system and generate electricity.

Insurgents gathering in Nad-e Ali presented an unwelcome distraction, if they attacked the convoy forcing the Brigade Commander to detach manpower from the Kajaki mission, there was a risk that the operation as a whole could be compromised. Any commander knows that he needs to win the propaganda war and getting the turbine in place would be a major coup. Success would mean 'lighting up' Helmand and a major boost for the hearts and minds campaign.

I'm leading a team of three medics and I feel responsible for the young Jocks that we are supporting. I am always mindful of the fact that every journey we make over the bomb-infested highways of Helmand might be the last for someone. Our job is to patrol Nad-e Ali and report back on the mood of the town and its people. If you find children playing outside their homes and people in the markets then 'atmospherics' are judged as good. If the streets are deserted, this paints a picture of uncertainty and often an attack of some kind is often imminent. The lead vehicles create a sand screen, which cuts our visibility.

I am top cover in our vehicle along with LCpl Kev Coyle. As top cover we give the driver and commander 360 degree eyes-on, scanning the ground we're passing over and the road ahead for potential threats. If there's an insurgent out there looking to take us on, the top cover usually gets hit first. I can taste the grit in my mouth that is being kicked up ahead of us.

Kev is B Company's signaller, he has an Italian look about him, jet black hair and olive skin. His bone dry sense of humour is an acquired taste, I had warmed to it through the hours we had spent together on the ground. 'This is fucking shite' Kev grunts. 'Aye, it doesn't look like we are stopping anytime soon either,' I reply.

'Eight more weeks pal, and that's us.' Our conversation is interrupted by an explosion, closer now a spiral of smoke rises into the air. Kev turns to me with a grin. 'Game on mucker' he whispers. I can read his lips over the noise of the engine and the bumps we keep hitting on the road. Kev and I had been battle buddies in an insurgent ambush down in the notorious district of Marjah. Sustained bursts of small arms peppered our vehicles and one of the lads took a round in the abdomen. Me and Kev had become firm friends ever since. Combat in close quarters wasn't how I thought it would be.

It felt strange and I remember having an overwhelming fear that I was about to be shot in the face. Our convoy consists of ten lightly armoured Land Rovers, consisting of the Snatch version and the open top WMIKs, which is short for Weapons Mounted Installation Kit. The WMIK is a stripped-down Land Rover that comes with a series of roll bars and special weapons mounts. It was designed primarily as a reconnaissance and fire support vehicle. The rear roll bar cage features a well in which a gunner can stand and swing his weapon in a 360 degree arc of fire around on a rail-mounted system.

The rear station can be fitted with a .50 calibre Heavy Machine Gun, a 40 mm Grenade Launcher or a 7.62 mm General Purpose Machine Gun (GPMG). American troops thought that we were crazy to be cutting about in open top vehicles. I explained that our guys were surviving IED attacks in WMIKs as they were being blown out of the vehicle compared to being thrown against the heavy armour inside the bigger vehicles.

The Snatch Land Rover, was in my opinion not so clever. It had been designed for tasks in Northern Ireland and was used in southern Iraq where UK troops used it in Basra. It was later shipped to Helmand and had been the focus of media controversy after numerous incidents in Iraq and Afghanistan.

It was not really ideal for Helmand and with its box body anyone inside would often boil, even with the later addition of air conditioning. In the brief before we left the Main Operating Base (MOB) we had been told that once we had completed the task we could make our way back to Lashkar Gah, which is the MOB where the Provincial Reconstruction Team is based. They are a joint team of Foreign Office staff and civilian advisors from the Ministry of Defence.

With military support they planned the strategic development and reconstruction of the region. I figured we'd be out of the base for 48 hours tops and packed my kit and equipment accordingly.

Back in the desert our vehicles continue to progress through the thick sand storm being whipped up by our convoy. I take in a face full of diesel fumes mixed with the dry, musky scent of the desert. The smell of diesel and hot air instantly reminds me of time spent in Iraq in the summer of 2003. In the stifling heat, I am thirsty and my is back soaking wet. To add to the situation my skull bakes like pie crust inside my helmet.

Afghanistan is land-locked in the bowl of the Hindu Kush, with mountains that go on forever. The landscape is severe, but beautiful and has a biblical feel to it. I'd served in Iraq, Kosovo, Sierra Leone, but Afghanistan isn't just another country. It's another mind set.

Winters are bleak and summers are marked by cloudless blue skies with temperatures topping 140 degrees. The dry climate and harsh environment has the ability to deliver beauty in the Springtime as the fields of Helmand blossom with red flowers. These fields harvest the 'death crop' of southern Afghanistan and while the opium poppies in full flower may present a picture perfect look, they have for many years funded war and criminality.

More than 90% of the world's heroin supply comes from poppies cultivated here. The country's illegal drug business generates $4 billion a year – half the nation's Gross Domestic Product. A big slice of that money buys the Taliban the guns that they use against us.

We often hear in briefings that 30 Taliban had been killed here, another 40 there. But they just keep coming in their dish-dashes and worn out shoes. We have the firepower. What they have is time. When we drive them out of different districts they flee to the mountains and wait. We pacify a town, maybe re-open a school. They come back when we leave and tear the building down again. They are like Hydra, the Greek mythical creature that had the ability to grow new heads. You kill a Taliban fighter and his eight brothers become new recruits for Jihad. We're fighting terror, they're doped up on a Holy War against us.

As our convoy comes to a halt on the outskirts of Nad-e Ali. The two platoon Sergeants, Monty Monteith and Scotty McFadden, get out of their vehicles and get among the tired and bored troops to ensure that all is as it should be. Monty and Scotty are firm friends. Monty's weathered appearance was a look reserved for the hardened soldiers of the infantry. Scotty seemed to have fared far better in avoiding the harsh '10 Years Older' weather of the Brecon Beacons beating on his face.

Brecon is a large training area in Wales used by the military. It is a place of outstanding beauty. The infamous land mark of the cattle-grid on Church Hill is where the fun begins for those venturing onto the Beacons. Wind, rain, sleet and snow accompanies the stunning backdrop. All that nature has to offer seems to come at you from every angle. There is something mesmerizing about being up and down those hills. When you stop for food or water your breath is taken away for a second time by the outstanding views that are visible from every miserable stinking treeline. Brecon is definitely a place to be enjoyed on foot.

Right now the boss, Major Harry Clark, is relaxed in the knowledge that both his Sgts are squaring things away on his behalf. With the Land Rover engines turned off I can hear a little more and listen to the sound of explosions across town.

We see black smoke rising and the distinctive rattle of sporadic small arms fire. It's no big deal and everyone on this patrol has seen and heard it all before. I climb down from top cover and sit in my pool of sweat feeling tired from the long day. Kev looks down at me. 'We should get some scoff on,' he says in an agitated voice. I hadn't realized until then that I was starving.

When you're tired, your sugar count gets low and your stomach starts to rumble. I was carrying biscuits brown and pâté, a light meal from my ration pack, which smells like cat food. It's not something I would normally choose, but right now I don't care. The Jocks have already eaten and are gobbing off, they are getting restless. I notice that Pte Scott Ferris and others are joking and taking the piss out of each other.

He, Ferris, is blowing kisses to the blokes on other wagons and making obscene gestures around his groin area, while manning his .50 calibre machine gun. The young Jocks fall about laughing, this was the norm around here and Ferris's antics are a welcome break. He managed to take my mind off my itchy wrists which were now starting to bother me. I have a rash caused by the fibre glass on top of the Snatch Land Rover, it slowly gets under your skin. Sitting back with my food and a cup of tea my mind drifts off. It was one of those moments when you're left nursing your own thoughts.

I was thinking about my time in Army Basic Training. Then I was always hungry, always drained. As recruit Taylor, I was constantly wondering at what level of degradation the instructors, the section commanders, would finally stop beasting us.

Every day that level got higher. Every day I felt like quitting and every day I decided I'd give it one more day. They take your dignity and you're not exactly sure what it is they give back in return. That doesn't become clear until much later. I was 22-years-old when I enlisted. I'd had a taste of life outside having worked in the retail industry since leaving school. I started as part of the old Youth Training Scheme and at the age of just 18 years I managed my own concession.

I had excelled at the visual merchandising aspect and was often rewarded for my efforts with trips on refit tasks up and down the country. I travelled as far up north as Manchester. Although I was a bit daunted with being away from home on my own, I quite liked the independent feeling it gave me. But my glory was short lived. The trips came to an abrupt end after my hotel bar bill far exceeded what it should have. This pushed me one step closer to my decision to sign up and join the Army. Growing up in the 1990's wasn't without its problems, there were a lot of distractions for a young boy or girl.

Ecstasy and the 'Mad-Chester' Happy Monday drug culture was rife and I along with everyone else got caught up in the glamour of it all. I would sometimes hide out in my bedroom listening endlessly to the Stone Roses' 'Waterfall' whilst inhaling on a bong, like my life depended on it. They were some of the darkest days of my life. For me, smoking Marijuana did not suit my personality. I became withdrawn and realised that this was definitely something to be avoided.

Gang violence along with the football hooligan culture was also prevalent. A sense of belonging to anything other than further education somehow made an awkward adolescence bearable. It's fair to say that I dabbled with a life in 'shitsville' and I didn't like it. Escaping it made me mentally tough and I somehow managed to drag my sorry arse (*pronounced ass*) kicking and screaming to the Army Careers Office. Every council estate or housing scheme across the UK is a 'target rich' recruiting area for the other ranks of the British Military.

Most soldiers hail from deprived areas and that's no bad thing. I was ambitious, without being sure where I was going and inquisitive about everything, without being sure what it was I wanted to know. All the doubt and arrogance was soon drummed out of me during the unknown number of hours I spent on my belt buckle crawling through the mud and cow shit.

More often it was running up and down the quarry hills at the Army Training Regiment Lichfield. We had the luxury of physical training instructors at Lichfield who also trained the young lads who wanted to be paratroopers, before they moved to the Infantry Training Centre at Catterick in Yorkshire. They took great pleasure in making sure we met the standard. You would never push yourself as hard or as far as the Army pushes you. You stop thinking like a civilian and start thinking like a soldier. I had grown up on a council estate, the youngest of five children, believing like an idiot that skiving off school was clever, it wasn't. The bravado that I engaged in as a teenager just camouflaged my lack of confidence.

I was definitely looking for something other than the humdrum of a conventional job. During basic training, I went through the mind-numbing day-in, day-out drills and instruction in a daze. In the end, I wanted nothing except to prove to myself I could do it. I came to see that becoming a proper soldier had taken me into a world where I could make my mark. I'd grown an inch taller straightening my back bone and I no longer lacked confidence, the curse of the working class. I saved lives and I was interested in everything. My day dreaming was interrupted as the order came to 'mount up' on the vehicles.

I was almost ready and quickly jumped aboard. The engines were running and we were on the move again. It is late and the orange sunset lasts only seconds before we are cast into twilight. Night Vision Goggles, NVGs, are fitted and night discipline begins. Orders have come down from higher command and we have been directed into the smoke and gunfire in the district centre of Nad-e Ali. My initial impression of atmospherics here are grim; plastic bags skipping down empty streets, that feeling of the calm before the storm.

Everyone in B Company feels it. They've got the look that Olympic high jumpers have before they sprint for the bar: determined and fully alert. It's the game on look Kev had noted earlier. Anticipation is sometimes worse than the actual event. You never know when or where it's going to happen. One thing that I am sure of is that I don't want it to be our wagon getting the good news first.

Flushed with adrenaline, I am no longer tired. I check that my medical kit is good to go. I forget my hunger and feel relieved that I don't have to eat my cat food. Not yet, anyway. We head towards the closed-down school, which is now the Nad-e Ali headquarters of an Afghan National Army Kandak – (Kandak means battalion in Dari, roughly 600 soldiers). They've taken several hits and are heavily undermanned.

Half the vehicles with Monty's platoon turn into the entrance where a group of Afghan soldiers stand about with expressions hard to read. The platoon will spend the night here showing them that we are willing to stand shoulder to shoulder with them.

The Kandak is commanded by Lt Col Nazim, a tough looking battle-hardened veteran who fought with the Mujahadeen many years ago against the Russians. With Major Clark, Scotty McFadden and the remainder of B Company, I press onto the Afghan National Police Compound, a sand-bricked building built around a courtyard in the centre of Nad-e Ali.

Travelling with our platoon is a Ford Ranger pickup packed with Afghan Police who are hanging onto the sides of the wagon with a one hand, the other holds an RPG launcher with a precarious finger curled round the trigger, which does not fill me with confidence. This isn't what we did in the British Army. Still, that's why we're here, to stimulate democracy and teach the fledgling Afghan Police and military the joys of battle discipline. The vehicles line up close to the wall inside the compound. As soon as we get out of the vehicles, LCpl Sean Maloney, un-clipping his chin strap, hurries across from his vehicle. 'Hey, Channy, it's Coaksee, he's sick,' he says. 'What?' I replied. 'Coaksee, he sick. With stomach. He look like shite.'

'No dramas, Sean, I'll be over in a minute,' I add. In spite of his Irish name, Sean's from the Caribbean and has developed his resemblance and persona of the rapper Dizzee Rascal in pursuit of the ladies. With his gangsta jargon, there are times when I think I need an interpreter to understand him.

However, having trained as an infantry soldier before becoming a combat medic I know that Sean has a lot to offer in times of trouble. The Jocks are shuffling about, checking weapons, pushing up onto the roof for better eyes on of the surrounding area. I watch the Afghan Police from our convoy jump out of their wagons. They look disinterested and shot to shit. To them this is just another day in Helmand Province. Meanwhile, Scotty McFadden and the boss are holding an impromptu meeting with the other unit commanders.

I find Private Gordan Coakes gritting his teeth leaning up against his WMIKs. As Sean had said, he looks like shit *(pronounced shite)*. Coaksee is your typical Jamsie Cotter type character from the BBC comedy 'Rab C Nesbit'. I know straight off he's embarrassed at needing attention. 'Alright, doll?' he says. As I pause for thought from nowhere someone screams: 'Incoming! Incoming!' Boom! Boom! Before I can reply, I'm scrambling around on the floor in the dark. Everyone's shouting, but the voices sound far away.

For a moment I can't understand a thing. I've been in contact before, when it kicks off you're always shocked, numb for a moment, disorientated. I check myself nothing missing. More explosions slam into the base as Rocket Propelled Grenades rain down on us.

They're coming in from two sides. You hear the thuds. The explosions drill into your ears and rattle your brain. A cloud of broken brick and dust fills the air, I can taste it. Another RPG drills into the wall opposite. I'm pinned down with Sean and Coaksee behind one of the wheels on the WMIK. I take hold of Coaksee's arm and the three of us scramble to get into the hardened part of the compound. I watch in disbelief as Major Clark and Scotty McFadden dodge their way across the open ground and climb the broken set of steps to the flat roof, they are open to enemy fire as they climb and the steps are already shot to pieces. On the roof they try to control the outgoing fire, within seconds they've organised the ramshackle Afghan Police who are engaging the enemy. Behind the rattle of our guns, I can hear the deep-throated roar of the Soviet made DShk, a 12.7 mm heavy machine gun. It's the Taliban's top weapon and for us it is the stuff of nightmares. If I wasn't sure before then the atmospherics now tell me that Nad-e Ali is on its arse. Rounds from semi-automatic weapons stitch holes into the walls.

Flashes of electric blue and green light made by the blasts illuminate the faces of two of the Afghan police who have taken cover with us in the building. They have blank, exhausted eyes. The enemy are Afghans. They're Afghans. There's no war like a civil war. We're outsiders, observers. We leave our blood in the Afghan dirt, but one day we'll be going home and they'll still have the same tribal conflicts they had long before the coalition arrived.

As for Coaksee, it's amazing what a shot of natural adrenaline can do for you. It draws out a peculiar energy. You fear death and feel reborn. He's got colour in his cheeks and joins the other blokes outside. My mind works overtime calculating how many casualties I think we are going to have and, if my calculations are correct, then we're fucked.

The barrage suddenly stops. I clamber to my feet. It didn't make sense. Either the Taliban had grown bored or they had gone to ground after receiving the good news from our guns on the roof. I am shocked to learn that by some miracle we have sustained no casualties. I don't ponder on what might have been. I check around the compound before making my way up the steps onto the roof. Searching for the boss I find him sitting behind a small brick wall relaying communications to Brigade HQ through Kev.

His eyes are bright in the dim light and there's dirt and dust covering his cheeks. 'We're good, Sir, no casualties,' I say. He returns a rare smile. Major Harry Clark is in his 30s, a tall man with carved features. He is well-educated and resolute, an officer with a stiff upper lip that never falters. He is passionate about his regiment and thinks before he speaks. 'Thanks, Sgt T,' he says simply.

That same moment, Monty's tobacco-thickened voice comes on the radio net from the old school. There's an exchange of call signs, then I hear my own. Monty has taken serious casualties and Abbie Cottle is treating them. 'My medic has four Cat B casualties.' 'How's she doing?' I ask quickly. I instantly know that Cat B means we need to get them to Camp Bastion as quick as possible.

'Best she can,' he says. 'She's worked on three. No breath sounds on one side of the fourth. You happy if she decompresses his chest?'

'Roger that' I reply.

'She wants your clearance.' He adds.

He asked knowing we had no doctor. I was the buffer for my medics. 'Tell her to crack on.' was my response. 'Roger that. Out'. This is a baptism of fire for Pte Abbie Cottle. A slim attractive brunette with something about her. She hails from Gloucester and embraces the twang of a southern accent.

She reminds me of when I was a junior medic and I have come to rely on her heavily already this tour. She chose Helmand as her first operational deployment. Cat B signifies that the casualties require urgent surgery. Four Cat Bs, even for an experienced medic, could prove overwhelming.

'Sir, these guys will need to be evacuated,' I advise the OC. Major Clark's been following the conversation and gives Kev Coyle the nod. Our signaller gets on the net to Brigade Headquarters at Lashkar Gah with a casualty report and we get the order to transport the injured to the Helicopter Landing Zone (HLZ) outside of Nad-e Ali. It would have been less detrimental for the injured men to bring the aircraft nearer the Afghan National Army base, but it was deemed too risky to land in what was an unknown area of operations for the pilots.

'Sir, are you happy if I take LCpl Young with me?' 'Yes, do.' he replies. It's encouraging in a crisis when everyone understands what everyone else has to do. It's not always that easy. The steps down to the compound are thick with dust and in my haste I slip hard on my arse. Jen hurries towards me. I tell her. 'You're coming with me to the school. Abbie has four Cat Bs over there'. I brush myself down whilst crossing the compound to the wagons.

Jenny is the fourth member of my team, a tall red head whose resilience and strength never cease to amaze me. She is quiet in character, an old school Northerner who only speaks if she has something intelligent to say. She doesn't waffle and just cracks on with the task in hand. We were here together on tour in back in 2006, then Jenny was a medic on the blue light ambulance, fetching casualties from helicopters and transporting our dead and wounded to the hospital in Bastion.

We're taking two WMIKs back to the ANA base. Instinctively, I climb into the vehicle with the biggest weapon, a .50 calibre machine gun, with Pte Michael Duffy cleaning dust off the barrel. The stuff is everywhere, thick as snow across the compound. It is just like talcum powder and gets everywhere up your nose, between the gaps in your teeth, in the corners of your eyes. 'You know how to work that .50 cal, Duffy?'

'Aye, you having a fuckin laugh?' Duffy smiles. Laughing at Duffy's response I explain : 'Four casualties at the school, we're moving them out to an helicopter site. 'Ne dramas, mucker.' He replies. Duffy is tall and slim, he has a typical runners build. Clean shaven and not growing a beard anytime soon on account of barely being out of short trousers. I remember Duffy from the MOB in Lash as an 18-year-old arsehole who listened to hard core rave music and drank too much Red Bull.

A loud, irritating kid. That was twelve hours ago. Like me, Mike Duffy could have taken a different path. He could have hung around on street corners feeling cheated, feeling like the world owed him a living. Instead he had chosen to serve his country and was now protecting me and my casualties. The engine starts up and we head off beneath the eerie light of the stars. My legs feel like jelly. The Taliban are out there, sons of the sons of the same resolute fighters that have always been there.

They say Afghanistan is the graveyard of Empires. They routed the Russians and the tribes kept the British from planting the Union Jack over Kabul. Alexander the Great in the 3rd century BC lost half his army in four years of battle and sealed the peace by marrying Roxana or 'Roshanak'. She was the daughter of a Bactrian named Oxyartes of Balkh in Bactria (the then eastern Achaemenid Empire, now northern Afghanistan, Uzbekistan and Tajikistan). She married Alexander at the age of 16 years after he visited the fortress of Sogdian Rock. Balkh was the last of the Persian Empire's provinces to fall to Alexander. Like most soldiers, I started to read about the history of the place before we deployed. History was telling me that everything we're doing has been done before and whatever mistakes were made then, we are making again.

Small arms fire rumbles through the night as we make our way to pick up the casualties. These Snatch Land Rovers and WMIKs which we are travelling in don't have sufficient under armour to deflect the bomb blast waves that can rip metal chassis and human bodies to shreds. While we've been pinned down in the compound the Taliban could have sown the road with IEDs. You don't know. Every metre, every minute, seems to take longer than normal.

'You're quiet Channy' Duffy says. I don't reply as for some reason I think that he is talking to someone else. He soon gets my attention. 'Fuck me, it's the morale police' he shouts.

Duffy's humour reminds me not to dwell too much on our situation and immediately brightens my mood. He slaps the barrel on his .50 cal. 'I'm gettin paid for this shite,' he says. At 18-years-old, Duffy appears to have no fear.

The roads are deserted except for some scrawny dogs that stand still as statues watching the vehicles pass. We make it to the Kandak base without incident. It was good to see Monty and hear his Jock welcome. 'Yous lot took yur fuckin time'. That's a good sign I thought, morale is high. Soldiers enjoy banter it takes their minds off the fact that they, like the four casualties, could be in a world of pain at any moment.

When you are accepted into the fold, you can expect insults involving a family member or worse still your mother doing something unmentionable. Through an open door I get a glimpse of Abbie Cottle at the centre of a group of Afghan soldiers. I follow Monty through the crowd. The moment he speaks, other conversations end. Monty has blue-grey eyes like chips of flint and a presence that leaves no doubt as to who's in charge. 'I've been keeping my eye on her,' he whispers to me. 'She's done well mate.'

As I enter the room where Abbie's been working I'm hit by the smell of gasoline, human shit and the cold coppery tang of blood. The four wounded are all Afghans, two have chest injuries and two of them have multiple shrapnel and fragmentation wounds. The five Afghans helping out as medical orderlies have lowered eyes and expressions that are both respectful and bewildered. This could well be their first encounter with a western woman. Maybe they've never seen the face of any woman except their mother before and the way they are willingly taking instructions from Abbie is an encouraging sign. They say in Afghanistan a woman should only leave her home twice in her life, the first time when she abandons her father's house to marry. The second time when she is taken from her husband's house to be buried.

Back in the room Abbie's drawn features tell me what kind of night she's been having. I move among the casualties checking that they are stable enough to fly. As I look up, Abbie's eyes meet mine. She has kept the four men alive in a situation that would have tested anyone. But Abbie is experienced, she was the first medic on scene when an IED killed Cpl Sarah Bryant and three reservists just weeks earlier.

I recall being very puzzled at the attitude of Brigade Staff after that hideous incident. News came through that we had lost four individuals including one female. Naturally my first thoughts were Abbie, and Jenny, my two medics who were both on taskings that day. Thankfully both were okay, but sadly Sarah had lost her life along with three lads Sean, Richie and Paul. Abbie was first on scene and was tasked along with the remainder of the patrol to guard the scene overnight. I would not see them until the next day. During breakfast I was told that all female soldiers working in the PRT were to report to the cookhouse at 0930 hrs for a 'lines to take' briefing. We were told that this was due to the heavy media presence in Lash. I took along my notebook and pen and waited patiently sitting on the tables outside the cookhouse. There were about eight other females in attendance and some who had shared accommodation with Sarah were visibly upset, comforting each other.

The incident had reminded us all that the Taliban did not discriminate when they plan their attacks. Out of the blue the Brigade Commander appeared. Shocked I wondered why the Brigade Commander was giving us a lines to take and media brief. Then all became clear. He embarked on a session of how morale on the base would be affected by the death of a female soldier and how it would affect us as females. Adding that how difficult it would be for us to lose one of our own. On and on it went.

I began to rage a little inside and switched my brain to selective hearing mode. I tuned out and didn't want to hear another word of what we were being told. The Brigade Commander wasn't the sort of man to take advice, he was very much a man's man and perhaps the fact that his career has been based around an all-male environment resulted in his misplaced compassion and concern. Sarah died as a soldier and I believed that she should be treated as one, she had earned that right by paying the ultimate price. I would later confide in Abbie that if something ever have happened to me then do not allow such an event to take place and tell my Mum that I was happy in my work. When the brief was over he asked if anyone had any points to make, my hand was quickly raised. He looked straight at me. Here was a man who had achieved great things.

He'd done more in his time in the military than I could ever care to imagine. But this time I felt that he had got it wrong and I needed him to know that I wasn't happy. So off I went. 'Sir, I want to make the point that should anyone at this table be asked about their feelings or opinions let's just remember that three guys died yesterday as well'. I stopped there as I could feel the Brigade Commander's eyes boring into me. 'Shit' I thought, waiting to hear his reply. I had mustered the courage to stare directly back at him and spoke with a clear unfaltering tone.

He replied; 'Yes good point'. It was the only point we should never have been sitting there and he knew it. If I could have said what I was really thinking then the conversation would have started with. 'If someone ginger dies, are you going to call everyone in with ginger hair for a debrief?' I could understand if we were a platoon or company group but none of us even worked together.

Clearly my better judgement stopped the ginger comment from ever crossing the threshold of my mouth. I was as sad as the next person to lose Sarah, but I was as equally sad about Sean, Richie and Paul. Any loss of life bears the same amount of grief and we all know that a family will be suffering at home regardless of sex, colour, or religion.

Our media have a habit of making one life seem more important than the next. Misogyny is always apparent throughout the ranks of the British military. Sometimes I agree with this train of thought and it is true that within the military not all places are designed for all women. On the flipside of that however, some places are not designed for all men and I have encountered plenty who don't come up to the mark, luckily for them though they hide amongst the majority.

The Afghan commander Lt Col Nazim appears, stern and patrician below his green beret. He says a few words in Dari and squeezes the shoulders of each of his injured men before we carry them out on makeshift stretchers to the wagons. 'Thank you, Sergeant,' he says to Monty, and turns bowing his head just slightly to Abbie. 'Thank you. Thank you.' The fleeting moment shared by the former Mujahedeen warrior and the young English woman is oddly moving. It brings into focus what we're doing here. The moment passes and I brief Abbie. 'Stay with this one' I tell her. 'We'll square away the others.' Her casualty is in shock, and needs attention. Abbie continues preparing him for evacuation. She has done all she can. The Jocks and the ANA cautiously place the stretchers on the wide floor space in the wagons. Battlefield wounds are hard to deal with at the best of times.

This is made all the more difficult when evacuating across rough ground. We make the wounded comfortable and carry out essential drills, checking tourniquets and dressings and ensuring that the intravenous drips are secure.

The Afghans and Brits are working as a team to prepare the wounded. Army training teaches you that the whole is greater than the parts. Afghan men are proud of their individuality and mark it with the way they arrange their headwear and shoulder their weapons. We set off in a four-wagon convoy past the hungry dogs out onto the pitch black road that runs along the side of the canal next to the old school. I finish another cigarette and promise myself I'll quit tomorrow remembering that I made the same promise on my last tour of Helmand.

Then I was supporting 3 Para Battle Group working long gruelling hours at the hospital in Camp Bastion. The medical facility was then one of the few permanent structures in a sprawling camp of blast blocks and razor wire carved out of the wilderness in what the locals call the Desert of Death. Our surgeons, nurses and the National Health Service (NHS) volunteers were pioneering new techniques and were saving more lives than ever, as the insurgency gathered pace in the summer of 2006.

The moon is high offering a fair degree of light outlining the tall vegetation running alongside the canal. In ten minutes we're at the helicopter landing zone and kill the engines. I step out of the vehicle. I'm wondering which way the helicopter is going to land. Is the doctor going to come off? Do they want the casualties on head or feet first? You're always worrying, listing problems, hoping for the best, expecting the worst. My eyes are strained from looking through the Night Vision Goggles (NVG) for so long. I should know to blink more often.

'Helo inbound' says Monty as he joins me, staring into the distance. I can see Abbie through the shadows kneeling by her casualty. I get eyes on the Chinook's glimmering rotor blades. I know the sound, the familiar whomph, whomph, the chug of the big engines.

The Chinook is an essential piece of kit for any war fighting army and I never stop being surprised that we have so few of them. Cylums - chemical lights - illuminate the ground. The blokes grab for the stretcher handles. The helicopter hovers above as it slows before setting down, the blades whipping up a storm.

Fuck! I've forgotten to tuck in my shirt and have to suck up the pain as a shower of grit hits my exposed lower back. The Chinook doesn't hang around. Our injured are loaded up. Two of the crew nod their heads as I hand over the paperwork.

It's all done in less than 30 seconds and the four Afghan soldiers are whisked away, back to the trauma unit in Bastion. I'm standing next to Monty. 'I should have asked if they were carrying any spare stretchers,' I said, putting word to my thoughts. 'We're going to need them.' He said. I turn to face him. 'Yeah right,' I say. ' But we'll be back in Lash tomorrow.' His brow crinkles. He had a certain look I'd seen before when you think you know your orders and someone else knows different. 'No, we're going to be stuck here for a wee while yet mucker,' he says.

The move back to the district centre of Nad-e Ali has everyone on edge. Using the same routes in and out of any hostile area makes our call sign vulnerable to an enemy ambush. Rubbing my hand across my lower back I feel the raw open grazes that were a gift as a result of my inability to tuck my shirt in during the casualty extraction. It's a minor injury but as my Osprey body armour gets to work on it, the pain is ever present. The move back goes by without incident. We roll back into the old school, which by now is bathed in light only from the high moon. I catch a quick word with Monty before the remainder of us push on to the Police Station. 'Stay safe mucker, I'll catch yous lot the morra'. Our two vehicles press on and my watch is telling me that I need sleep, today feels like it is never going to end.

The Police Station is in darkness the only noise coming from the engines of our WMIKs. Duffy dismounts from his position on the .50 cal. 'I'm Fucked' he grunts. I am too tired to offer any response, my body aches from being crammed in the back of the vehicle. I feel my soaked shirt under my body armour and lap up the smell of dry blood. Jumping down from the tailgate I grab my kit, slinging my weapon on my back.

Scrambling up the dusty, barely there, shot to shit steps onto the roof. I make my way over to check in with Major Clark our OC. He acknowledges our return. 'Everything alright Sgt T?' asks the boss.

'All good Sir, everything went smoothly'. I almost forget the deep grazes now covering my lower back. I look for a space to settle down for a few hours, there are bodies strewn all over the place its cold on the roof as there is very little shelter as it is exposed to the fresh winds coming in from the open desert a few kilometres north of Nad-e Ali. The town of Nad-e Ali sits in the West of Helmand Province. Much of the district is unoccupied desert with the bulk of population living in the East, near the provincial capital Lashkar Gah. This district thrives on its opium trade with a high percentage of the profits going directly to officials in Kabul. The local people are not overly supportive of the Coalition, they know that it's only a matter of before we leave.

Still searching for somewhere to sleep, I spot our interpreter sleeping soundly in his bulky 'Army issue' sleeping bag. He has sensibly packed the issued 'bouncing bomb'. It is a huge sleeping bag, which is issued back in the UK but rarely used by troops because of its inoperable size . It can easily fill a bergen and sensibly I left mine behind.

When I packed my kit I took my bivvy bag which is basically a protective outer layer for the proper sleeping bag. It is thin, offers little comfort and yes I am now regretting my decision. Mumbling with discontent I climb into my bivvy and try to get comfortable, my overtired brain keeping me awake. I suffer a further hour of the cold and a series of 'what if' this or that happened problems in my mind, before I decide to adopt the spoons position behind our interpreter. This will at least afford me some of his body heat. He's asleep and doesn't even realize that I am there. When he wakes he will presume that it's one of the blokes and for that reason alone he won't be too bothered. What's left of the cold night flashes by, at dawn we stand to. When first light comes it is usually accompanied by some form of attack, the Taliban have had the night to manoeuvre and plan what for them will be another day's paid work. For them payments include $10 a day for local young men to join their fight against the infidels.

This is of course all in the name of Allah and for many too good an offer to turn down. As quick as the landscape is exposed by the sun, my attempts to stay warm offer the blokes around me some much needed laughter and a morale boost. Kev is the first to applaud my resourcefulness. 'Smooth operator mucker, ne flies on you Channy eh?' he says.

'Aye Kev, am shocked you weren't in the bag wi him ya wee fanny', says Scotty Mcfadden as he joins in the banter. Jocks to the left of me have eyes on a group of fighting aged males less than 200 yards from the base as the morning routine signifies the end of our stand to.

The group of males have disappeared allowing the young Jocks to get busy cleaning weapons and preparing themselves for the day ahead. Boil in the bag rations are eaten cold and I tuck into my cat food and biscuits that up until now I had managed to avoid. It's not long before Monty joins us from the old school. He undertakes a vital role within B Company and heads straight to Major Clark for an impromptu set of orders. Scotty and the Sgt Major are also in attendance as our mission suddenly changes. The trip back to the luxury of Lashkar Gah is no longer happening.

Our so called 48 hr operation is a thing of the past. B Company has now received new orders and it looks like we are here for a while longer.

We are to move in convoy to the old school enabling support to what is left of the Kandak. We will stay there until further notice. I sort my equipment out and make some notes about medical supplies we are going to need as it becomes clear that we are here for a while. Before leaving Monty notices one of the junior officers has placed a belt of 7.62 ammunition upside down onto one of the guns. 2Lt Barclay who would later be awarded the Military Cross for bravery, is the offending officer. He is verbally chastised to the delight of the Jocks, five or more of them making the squawking sound of a crow, as the rest are in bits laughing their heads off.

The area housing the WMIKs is a hive of activity. Wagons are squared away and the Company   is preparing to move. Young Duffy is busy checking his much loved .50 cal, I take time to clean my own weapon and check my medical kit before mounting up with Kev and Major Clark.

'Cpl Coyle are we good to go?' The boss asks 'Roger that Sir' Kev replies giving a wry smile. We set off towards the old school, small arms fire ever present in the distance. This would turn out to be the least kinetic move that we would experience over the next two months.

CHAPTER TWO

Afghan Fighting

The Company arrived at the Afghan base in darkness. The place looked different to what I could recollect from yesterday. It was scruffy and makeshift, displaying all the sign of a base under siege. Afghans soldiers sat around, some smoking, others sleeping and chatting. They look shattered and we are quickly informed that they have been under the cosh for several weeks, constantly engaged in fire-fights with the Taliban. They have lost men and are low on food and ammunition. We hear that these men have been involved in hand to hand combat and many looked dejected. Their battle worn faces said it all.

The Afghans had been fighting on their own and in difficult situations. They had no indirect fire weapons such as artillery and have not been afforded the luxury of Close Air Support (CAS) in the form of the Apache or fixed wing fighter aircraft that Coalition forces can call upon. Fighting the Taliban had become a daily routine for these guys – it was just another day at the office.

These men are fierce and proud fighters. But many lacked the basic instinct that British soldiers learn in training of making sure that their kit is looked after, they were in disarray and their battle discipline was non-existent. Their body armour was all over the place, weapons leant up against walls in direct sunlight, rubbish was strewn everywhere and the smell of human faecal matter was so strong it was overpowering the diesel fumes from our vehicles.

Davey Robertson, B Company's Sergeant Major set about 'claiming' some real estate so his men could get straight into a routine. He is an old school soldier with a strong character and by all accounts is a bit of a hard bastard, I am yet to see any takers put this to the test. At just under six feet tall Davey is covered in old tattoos, he has a glint in his eye, just like my man Duffy.

His happy hardcore music would have probably been the Jam or ACDC. That's how it works, generations may change but we all had our struggles somewhere along the line. It's called common ground, that's how people in the military get on. You may not like the guy standing next to you but you will find a purpose with him to ensure that the job gets done. I have only ever seen that in the army and more often than not you grow to like someone's once annoying habits. It is just the way it is, team work.

Monty and Scotty get busy placing troops into defensive positions ensuring all arcs – where the Taliban might attack from – are covered (the idea of this is that base will have 'all round defence' should the worst happen and the Taliban mount an assault.)

An Afghan Army position on the roof of the tallest building is reinforced with a heavy machine gun. The big .50 calibre machine guns can be dismounted from vehicles and placed where they can be used most effectively when the troops are not on patrol. This job is left in the capable hands of Cpl Scotty Pew. Scotty is a young section commander. He is physically and mentally tough and his section have the back breaking job of carrying sandbags up onto the roof to reinforce it from attack. This is a physical and time-consuming job. Sand bags are filled and Pew and his team carry them one by one up the dodgy steps to the gun position on the roof, which just happens to be riddled with 7.62 mm holes from earlier fire-fights with the enemy.

The Taliban would have eyes on the position at all times. Scotty Pew and the other young Scots were happy that the enemy knew they were there. For the young Jocks it now meant that the Taliban could see the fire power that would smash them in any future attack. Private Drew Elder is another young soldier busy on the roof.

Elder was issuing Fire Control Orders last night to the less experienced Jocks, acting as platoon runner for Scotty. He was relaying information from one area of the roof to another and took on the role as 'link man' for the platoon.

The platoon link man is probably the single most important job in any fighting unit, if Elder gets it wrong the platoon or company can become ineffective very quickly. Elder was raised in Falkirk, he's learning fast that his job is a thankless sometimes perilous task. He puts his life on the line with every step taken in his role as link man. Every man has a job to complete before any contemplation of rest is realised. Major Clark's communications are set up by LCpl Kev Coyle and he quickly turns an unused classroom into a Company Command Post. Kev has the unenviable chore of keeping this Company in communication with Brigade Headquarters.

I stop my own job of setting up a makeshift Company Aid Post for a much needed drink of water. I look around at the young soldiers going about their business when it suddenly dawns on me that not so long ago some of them would have been standing on street corners of Glasgow and other cities sipping from bottles of Buckfast tonic wine. They would have gone through the same decisions that I had before signing up.

Many were from broken homes, or they had crossed to and from the wrong side of the tracks. Colourful backgrounds are in abundance throughout the ranks of most armies. To me this was nothing to be ashamed of, if anything it brings character to the army and that is exactly what we need if we were to stand any chance of holding Nad-e Ali. The young Jocks were now manning the corners of this isolated Patrol Base poised to introduce the Taliban to a 'Glasgow kiss' in the shape of a .50 calibre machine gun. The only drink in sight is bottled water or a few cans of Red Bull that the lads had managed to squeeze into their vehicles or bergens. When it comes to fighting these men do it with ease, they are steeped in an infectious lust for life and they are hardened beyond their years. Their instinct to survive comes from a history of ferocious fighting men.

As I make my way back into the ops room the team are busying themselves emptying two patrol medical packs. We operate a military medical assessment using the MARCH -P principals:

M – Massive Haemorrhage.

A – Airway.

R – Respiratory/Chest.

C – Circulation.

H – Head Injury/Hypothermia.

P – Pain/Evacuation

It differs from our civilian counterparts, as a massive haemorrhage will kill someone on the battlefield long before a blocked airway. We use tourniquets far more freely in our line of work and it would seem that the conflicts in Iraq, Mogadishu and Afghanistan are helping the medical world to adopt new protocols when dealing with traumatic injuries.

As combat medical technicians we carry battlefield trauma bags and small primary health care packs. Extensive training followed by even more extensive live tissue training best prepares medics for types of injuries seen in war. Having said that nothing prepares you for your own reaction. I have three junior medics in my charge so the two remaining patrol packs will be used when members of the trauma team deploy outside the wire.

As lead medic I answer to the boss and advise him on all matters concerning his men and their wellbeing. There is no room for error, I had been waiting for this my whole life. Could I make this work? Could I deliver under pressure or would self-doubt cripple me? Ultimately could I live with the prospect of letting these men down? Anyone who puts their head above the pulpit opens themselves up to the chance of failure. We are in our third month of Helmand and as a team we work effortlessly.

There is no room for egos on this deployment. One minute you could be taking orders from higher command and the next you might have to step up and deal with situations that far exceed your pay scale or rank. I covered the Medical Desk in Brigade Headquarters, a job usually taken on by a senior Captain or Major. On my first day a mass casualty call came in, I had to quickly evaluate and decide what assets were required and make the necessary arrangements for evacuation. This made all the more complicated by the fact that the injured were local nationals.

My moment of truth was played out under the watchful and very skilled eye of the Brigade Commander. The pressure I felt was huge, but I was determined not to falter. He was also the sort of bloke who would have not said anything to me if I was making a hash of things. He would have just told the Chief of Staff to sack me or move me on somewhere.

As the hours passed the heat increased, my overzealous start to the day had left me hungry. I tuck into more of my ration pack pate and biscuits, then make my way into the operations room again to help Kev tape up the windows using black bin liner bags to drown out any light. Light from the smallest source travels far and drawing attention to the room could have disastrous consequences.

Basic battle discipline was the only way to survive here. The atmosphere around the base is one of trepidation. On the opposite side of the patrol base is the area housing the Afghan Army, they look on inquisitively as western forces continue to turn their ramshackle base into a workable fortress in minimal time. My peripheral vision witnesses a flash of movement , it is a group of Afghan soldiers who dive for cover as I hear the initial crack of incoming rounds.

Taliban rounds slam into the base punching small holes into the walls and sandbags. Kev sends the initial contact report and already the heavy machine guns on the roof are letting rip, pounding the enemy positions. The sound is deafening making it hard to tell the difference between outgoing and incoming fire. Monty and Scotty are directing our fire with bursts of .50 calibre , Heavy Machine Gun, rounds stopping only to allow the distinctive crack of the 7.62 mm General Purpose Machine Gun.

Amid the noise and chaos, the boss, Major Clarke, tries hard to control his men, issuing direct orders for the link man Elder to carry to the roof. Under heavy fire Elder sprints off into the clouds of sand and broken brick thrown up by the rounds pumping into the buildings. He returns with news of what and who is being engaged from the roof.

Cpl Scotty Pew has eyes on ten or more enemy fighters, they are using the canal and compounds as cover and are moving freely between tree lines and overgrown fields. He has engaged them with several bursts from the .50 cal. The rounds from this weapon system are the same size as a thick felt tip pen, you don't want to be on the receiving end of one.

Within ten minutes, five enemy fighters are confirmed dead, an Apache has arrived on station and is now hunting Taliban targets from the sky. This strange looking hi-tech helicopter has the profile of a 'preying-mantis'. The Apache is the biggest success story in Helmand and in military terms it is a force multiplier as it can deliver the firepower of a support weapons company and more with just two air crew, a chain gun and a pile of missiles. It's not long before this engagement starts to appear one sided. With no reports of friendly casualties the balance had been tipped and nine Taliban are confirmed dead. We thought it was all over and just as the situation had started to calm down it kicked off again. The blast seemed louder than usual and from my position I see a flash and feel the shock wave from the explosion. It's close this time, far closer than I would like. Something has been hit, I wait for more explosions thinking that it may be incoming mortar rounds when someone shouts 'incoming'.

This is quickly followed by Kev's dry retort of 'No shite Sherlock'. He looks across and gives me a nod of approval that our taped up window job had achieved its aim. No inward blast luckily for Kev, it would have taken him out as he sits relaying information to Brigade Headquarters.

A voice screams 'Medic! Medic!' When the dreaded call comes, it always sounds desperate. The base is silenced. Jenny and I sprint outside and almost collide with the boss, he drags us to the outer wall where Cpl Tony McParland was firing from, it's a short distance so we are there within a few steps. My stomach is churning and I dread what I will find, no incident is ever the same so the systematic approach to treatment must happen without delay. Tony's body is twisted and I spot a mangled hand with fingers missing. I am relieved that it is only fingers and not limbs. Like clockwork our treatment begins. He is already in enough cover so no movement is required. I talk through each section of MARCH in my head being sure not to miss a single thing. My assessment takes less than 60 seconds and we get the all important tourniquet applied. It's care under fire so the assessment must be quick and I am lucky to have time to carry out any medical interventions. It's not long before the sound of small arms has us dragging Tony into the cover of the Company Aid Post.

Once there my next move is to identify the need for early surgery. More often than not injuries sustained on the battlefield require minimal first aid and super quick evacuation to the hands of the highly skilled surgeons in Camp Bastion, the main operating base for Coalition forces in Helmand Province.

Jenny dresses the wound before Tony sees it. Noise from the guns above make it hard to concentrate and the failing light starts to offer up its own set of problems. I relay to Kev that we have at least one Category B, which signifies that he is an urgent surgical case and has life/limb threatening injuries. The UK military have an established system to prioritise injuries into three groups, which indicate to everyone involved the urgency of their injuries, they are;

Cat A is life threatening and the casualty requires urgent medical treatment.

Cat B Is life threatening and casualty urgent surgical treatment.

Cat C is non life threatening and can be held for up to four hours.

Kev initiates what we call a Nine Liner to Headquarters. This the set of nine questions that are answered by call signs on the ground and sent up via the radio net to Brigade Headquarters.

These questions are then assessed at the medical desk and a decision made which will see a instant response if relevant or a timely extraction depending on the in jury. The Nine Liner is used by all UK medical teams on operations and provides vital information to the chain of command. The nine statements are;

Line 1. Location of the pick-up site.

Line 2. Radio frequency, call sign, and suffix.

Line 3. Number of patients by precedence:

Line 4. Special equipment required:

Line 5. Number of patients:

Line 6. Security at pick-up site:

Line 7. Method of marking pick-up site:

Line 8. Patient nationality and status:

Line 9. Contamination:

While I have assessed that Tony is stable, I do not have the luxury of a CT scan and would never assume that something far more sinister isn't going on. An X-ray Computed Tomography or CT scan is a medical imaging method employing tomography to create a 3-D image of the inside of an object.

To you and me it's a body scanner hunting for abnormalities or potential bleeds that aren't showing on the outside.

The trouble with treating physically fit soldiers is they can often disguise severe injury until it's too late. Their fit bodies will sometimes mislead medics into thinking that all is well. The body is an amazing piece of engineering, it's designed to shut down and protect itself. It will fool an untrained eye in to thinking all is well before freefalling at a rapid rate. I remember my time in Sierra Leone an officer literally walked away from a helicopter that had crash landed. She died minutes later from an internal bleed. We treat for the worst and hope for the best possible outcome. A close encounter with an RPG rocket propelled grenade does not leave a healthy outcome in anyone, so with an air of caution I administer Tony 10 mg of Morphine. If it's IM intramuscular it could take up to 30 minutes to take effect.

An IM medication is given by needle into the muscle. This is as opposed to a medication that is given by a needle, for example, into the skin (intradermal) or just below the skin (subcutaneous) or into a vein (intravenous). Medics are issued with morphine auto jets each holding a one hit dose of 10 mg. I have never been a fan of this system; it's easier to monitor a patient's progress if the morphine is given intravenously or into the vein. It can be titrated (diluted) therefore faster acting and less likely-hood of overdose. This process in my view can be very helpful.

In 2006, there were cases where Surgeons in Bastion were dealing with morphine overdoses before getting stuck into the actual wounds. My own theory on the administration of morphine is that a little pain lets a casualty know that he is still alive and better still it lets me know that he is alive.

I can manage a casualty easily if he is still with it. If the security situation goes tits up his treatment will stop until our safety is re-established. Titration of morphine is the way forward and most forward operating medics live by this and many of the grunts on the ground often refuse morphine until I explain how I will administer it. No one wants to lie helplessly in such a hostile environment. Without warning Tony starts to act erratically, had I misjudged the severity of his head injury? For a second I question myself. My own pulse increases and all of a sudden my palms are sweaty. I look deep into Tony's eyes with my torch and re-assess the wound. I check behind his ears, up his nose and look for anything that I may have missed. Thankfully, my panic is short lived as Platoon Sgt Scotty McFadden comes in and tells Tony to 'Man up and stop acting like a fuckin lunatic'. Tony starts to laugh. I put my own sense of humour failure on hold and get on with the task in hand. Just to add to my now irritated state Abbie and Sean come running into the Company Aid Post with three more casualties.

All have multiple shrapnel wounds; one in particular requires urgent surgery to a wound penetrating his abdomen. We now have a potential mass casualty scenario and the Nine Liner is quickly updated.

All casualties are stabilised and as my team finish off preparing our injured for evacuation I disappear into the ops room to update the boss and get a wheels up time from Kev. Wheels up, is the time that the rescue bird will leave Camp Bastion. This allows me and the team time to manoeuvre our injured out to a helicopter landing zone.

The attack came at last light, an age old tactic adopted by every fighting force since the days of Ghenghis Khan and the Romans. The Taliban are creatures of habit and generally attack from positions that have been successfully used before, this was used time and time again to systematically slaughter the Russian occupiers during the late 1970's early 80's. It ensures that the attack is on their terms and at a time of their choosing. They also know the area and all potential escape routes including ours. In military terms it's all about controlling the battle space, another piece of useless information I had picked up during my time on the Medical Desk. Again another from 2006 is the fact that our government believed that we could control Helmand with less than 4,000 troops.

We sent 40,000 to Iraq and by 2008 we had around 8,000 soldiers in southern Afghanistan - the most dangerous place on the planet. I did not need a university degree to realise that we may have underestimated just how many Jihadists we were taking on.

News from Camp Bastion says that wheels are up and the MERT (Medical Emergency Response Team) helicopter is inbound. The MERT offers our casualties a lifeline. They are the unsung heroes of the battle to secure Helmand. The team is made up of highly qualified medical personnel who are capable of giving in-flight lifesaving treatment if and when required.

Sgt Major Robertson hastily leads a patrol from our base to secure the route to and from the helicopter landing zone. The chosen site is an old football pitch opposite the base on the other side of the canal. All of this is happening under the cover of darkness and the young Jocks rely heavily on the basic low-level soldiering skills, which cover movement at night. With technology ever moving forward it is sometimes easy to forget the basics. My team are on foot and carrying four extremely heavy casualties. Davey relays via a runner and confirms that the landing site is secure, my extraction team are ready and we prepare to move. The evacuation must be measured at all times with clear command and control.

My role only ends when my casualties are airborne until that time I must keep a grip on the situation. Hearing the sound of the Chinook in the distance. My mind is buzzing with questions to myself as I mentally check that I have covered everything.

Which way it is going to land? Are we at the right end of the football pitch? Are my casualties stable enough? Who am I going to hand over to? My list is endless, no one can answer my questions, my heart races again, my pulse is raised and my sweaty palms ever present. The Chinook comes in low and fast, touching down amid a huge cloud of dust. On the ground the cool night air on my face is quickly warmed by the downdraft of the powerful double engines to the rear of the aircraft.

A small green light in the back allows me to identify the crewman and gives me a path to follow with my casualties. I give the hand over notes to whoever is available and then ensure that all of my team are off before waving to the door gunner. It was painless and went perfectly, just as we like it. As the Chinook takes off my team take cover the downdraft almost blowing me over. 'Good positioning Taylor' I think to myself as I re-run the Chinook's landing in my head. We double back to the safety of the patrol base. All command elements gather in the ops room for hasty orders.

Here we learn that the word from headquarters is that we are going to be here for the foreseeable future. We are not heading back to Lashkar Gah. Clearly some staff officer in Brigade has concerns about the tactical situation in Nad-e Ali. We will struggle with our small number to provide total security. All the Jocks can do is kill as many Taliban as they can and attempt to cripple the enemy's grip on the area.

Major Clark, is concerned about Cpl McParland and Colonel Nazim, the Afghan commander, is worried about his men. I reassure them both that I didn't envisage any major problems, however any number of complications could occur. The balance of survivability was definitely in our favour, all we could do was wait for news from Bastion. Another long day culminating in a casualty evacuation has left every man exhausted. I look around the medical room and ponder the questions that I often have that are never answered, the silent wide-eyed panic stricken faces the same as I am probably wearing myself. How were people reacting to combat stress and fatigue? In just 48 hours so much had already happened.

The base was unsafe and the blokes had yet to patrol out of it. I knew then that these men would come to rely heavily on me and my team. All of us knew our place in B Company that night.

I longed for a decent night's sleep, but not before cleaning up the mess that had been left by our injured. One thing was for sure, we hadn't seen the last of spilt blood so our medical room was prepared to receive again. My attention was rapidly turned as I overhear a conversation between the boss and the Kandak Commanding Officer.

It turned out that the direct hit from the rocket propelled grenade had come from inside the base. An Afghan soldier had fired low from one of the roofs. Cpl Tony McParland had been manning the outer wall when he was struck by the RPG round. The news wasn't welcomed by the Jocks at all. This wasn't the best start to relations between the two sets of soldiers. Amazingly the soldiers took the news in their usual relaxed stride. 'Cunts' was echoed around the patrol base for the rest of the evening. The fact was Tony could have been killed.

When all was said and done the young Jocks knew that they had to fight alongside the Afghan Army if they were to stand any chance of surviving down here. The Afghan fighters were as knowledgeable as the Taliban when it came to knowing the ground and terrain, their input was priceless and it was our job to mentor them and introduce them to battle discipline. They had a medical team just like us and I was happy to work alongside the ANA.

I finish what is probably a whole packet of cigarettes, not bad for a non-smoker. My throat is parched as I down two bottles of water one after the other. I need sleep and look down with less than eager eyes at my thin roll mat and my even thinner bivvy bag.

A quick brush of teeth and I lay my head for the night. I think about what will become of us and still have hope that we may return to Lashkar Gah tomorrow. The town of Lashkar Gah sits in the heart of Helmand, it is the capital and seat of the Provincial Afghan government. The base is in the centre of a heavily populated area and is home to the UK Task Force Commander. I had flown into Lash when I had arrived 12 weeks earlier on a Chinook, after initially landing in Kandahar aboard a Tristar.

I had been here briefly back in 2006, but there had been big changes. The deployment of UK military forces in Lash followed a tradition for the area. Lashkar Gah is 'Army Barracks' in Persian. The town developed a thousand years ago as a riverside barracks town for soldiers accompanying the Ghaznavid nobility to their grand winter capital of Bost. The ruins of the Ghaznavid mansions still stand along the Helmand River; the city of Bost and its outlying communities were sacked in successive centuries by the Ghorids, Genghis Khan, and Timur Leng.

Today the nearby hamlet of Bost is home to a hospital and airport. Back in Nad-e Ali, the old school has thick walls that offer more warmth than that of the roof from last night. The as if someone had just pressed the fast forward button on a shite Betamax video machine, the glow of the morning sun is already upon us. I manage to get four hours sleep although it felt more like two.

B Company stands to as the sun rises over Nad-e Ali. In normal circumstances this would be my favourite time of day. The sky is serene and beautiful it makes good the sometimes harsh landscape. The muezzin call to prayer signifies the end of stand to. The muezzin, a man appointed to call to prayer, climbs the minaret of the mosque, and calls in all directions. Many mosques no longer require the muezzin to climb the minaret. Instead, a loud speaker carries the message.

The mundane but necessary chores of morning routine are a welcome break from taking cover. My bladder feels like it is about to explode and I don't know the last time that I emptied it. Stumbling outside I search the nearby vehicles for my multi-purpose yellow sharps container. This small piece of kit has afforded me the luxury of a portable toilet for the last five months. I climb into the back of my vehicle and keep my dignity by balancing over the sharps container out of sight of the base.

I am stuck in what now feels like a stress position for an absolute eternity thighs burning, still not finished. Moments like this make me wish that I had joined the Royal Air Force. I eventually finish, laughing for a second at my efforts trying to stand up. Sleeping rough has left me with a few minor aches and pains. I accidently smash my head on the roof of the vehicle as I manoeuvre myself around. Even wearing the cumbersome Mark 6 Alpha helmet doesn't stop the vibrations going straight to my skull. I need to wash my hands, but water is scarce, I pull my packet of wet wipes out of my map pocket and try to wipe away the grime and remnants of what looks like blood from my hands. Hunched over in the back of the wagon I pull up my trousers. I take a small clear bag from the top of my basic wash kit and use it as a makeshift trash bag. It's these basic traits that make life bearable in a place like Nad-e Ali.

If your personal administration is poor then you will not survive too long in these conditions. My time teaching raw recruits all about basic field admin had reminded me how to deal with myself. After two years of showing them how to do it I found this part easy, lack of sleep was becoming my biggest challenge. My final chore is to brush my teeth, while I have no concerns about the rest of my body as that won't stop me functioning, my teeth however might.

It's all down to personal preference and my morale is instantly lifted when I have clean hands and teeth. My rumbling stomach signifies that I haven't eaten for quite some time and my stained grubby combats have become a little baggier around the waist.

I dig out my ration box from my day sack and start to look inside at the culinary delights that I will be enjoying today. British Army rations are for sustainability only. They aren't known for their Michelin star rated menus, perhaps I am being a bit harsh.

At times like this I would give anything for an American ration pack or Meals Ready to Eat as they call them. They include M&Ms and lemon pound cake. Not today though, corn beef hash and beans for breakfast it is! I am starting my day well as things can only improve from this. It's not long before all command elements are summoned to the ops room for routine orders. This would become a regular event regardless of the time of day or night.

This Patrol Base wasn't going to maintain itself and the boss needed to be confident that everyone in his team understood what was expected of them. The company will be sending out its first patrol later today, Sgt Scotty McFadden will lead his multiple of men to meet a Combat Logistic Patrol (CLP) coming from Lash with a re-supply.

As soon as the word re-supply is mentioned it became clear that we were staying for longer than any of us had expected. The main operating base in LKG will be a ghost town with the majority of its force protection down here in Nad-e Ali. What's strange is I am not as disappointed as perhaps I should be. In some crazy warped way I had hoped that we would revisit the badlands of Marjah, which lies south of Nad-e Ali. Myself and Kev had often joked about the 'Battle for Marjah' having already felt the buzz of adrenaline that comes with close quarter engagement.

The mixture of fear and excitement left us naively wanting a little more. As it goes a new story was emerging 'The Battle for Nad-e Ali'. This is what I thought that I had signed up for and I didn't want to be back in Lash listening to someone else's war stories. Nad-e Ali had a different atmosphere to LKG it was raw Taliban country I felt excited, nervous and scared all at the same time. Above all it was an experience that I had started to enjoy in a strange, almost macabre way. I wondered why I was drawn to such a clearly unstable situation and just looking around I saw that we all were. The fear felt healthy, it wasn't the same as a fear of heights it was a fear that needed a reaction and the reaction was bringing the best out in people, well so far anyway.

The last 48 hrs had given us only a glimpse of what was yet to be thrown our way. Scotty's platoon, we call it a multiple, start preparing themselves and their vehicles for the upcoming patrol. They will leave under the cover of darkness, I assign Jenny Young to Scotty's patrol. She has spent the last four months with these guys and is more than capable of any such task. Myself, Abbie and Sean set about establishing a bonafide Company Aid Post or CAP preparing a wish list to send across the radio net back to Lash. Going by the casualties that we have taken so far I order above and beyond what would normally be required.

As lead medic with no doctor here, my responsibilities include the provision of a mass casualty and evacuation plan. Patients must be categorized correctly at all times as this will ensure that the distribution of medical assets at Brigade HQ level happens efficiently and without unnecessary delay.

My secondary task on the Patrol Base is to assess environmental health issues, it's not glamorous but a fundamental part of camp set up and routine. My first task takes me to the toilet block that has been allocated to B Company, I get within five metres of the mud brick walls and start to dry heave on account of the smell. The block comprises of five single cubicles each containing a single hole into the ground below.

On the back wall of each cubicle was a head height window looking straight over the perimeter wall and out into Taliban country just like a murder hole. Already I imagine the scene of getting shot in the face, while squatting over the hole. I shake my head and laugh as the blokes guarding that corner of the Patrol Base, encourage that exact same thought before I had a chance to share my own with them.

'Hey Channy, fancy getting shot in there and one of us has to come and get you out' 'That works both ways eh mucker' I reply laughing acknowledging the fact that they are the lucky ones sleeping next to the shitters. I make my way back to the ops room to report my findings to Company Sergeant Major Davey, he shakes his head and smirks when I tell him he should crouch down whilst squatting to avoid the murder hole.

After one trip to the toilet Davey manages to acquire an old wooden chair removing the seat he creates a makeshift toilet bringing a much needed laugh and morale boost to the team on that corner. The day seems to have gone by in a flash and with most tasks complete the base is yet again plunged into twilight as last light looms. 'Stand to' orders are given. Like clockwork the rounds start flying again and this time the Taliban appear to be concentrating heavily on our gun positions.

Medi, the Afghan soldier who fired the RPG gunner from last night waits patiently to redeem himself. With no target acquired he is stood down from any type of RPG action much to the relief of the Jocks on the wall. The attack isn't sustained and there are no casualties to report. Scotty's platoon mount up under the command of 2Lt Alexander Barclay. As they leave the patrol base I take the time to relax in the medical room, Davey and Monty discuss possible options for Nad-e Ali and who would come to support B Company.

Eating some biscuits fruits from my ration box. I opt for lying out on one of the stretchers and join in the discussion by adding: 'Which medic do you want to come and get you if you get shot in the toilet block?' An overwhelming majority announces 'Sean will come and get us and you can see us back in here.' Our idle but morale boosting chat is interrupted as the radio net becomes busy and we can hear all of the traffic from next door. Scotty's multiple has touched base with the Combat Logistic Patrol sent from Lashkar Gah. Kev relays all information to the boss without exception. The convoy are making their way back to the Patrol Base.

The constant fear of an IED strike is never far away. The Taliban plant them at will through the night and we find them one way or the other the following day or a week from now.

Hoping for a day without an significant event in Nad-e Ali is at best never going to happen. Within minutes of moving off the convoy is in serious trouble. A desperate sounding voice is heard over the net and instantly gets our attention.

'Hello Topaz Zero Alpha, this is Topaz Two Zero we have a vehicle down, I say again we have a Vehicle down'.

The net is frantic and the mood in the ops room suddenly changes, Major Clark is desperate for information and the gravity of the situation on the ground is yet to be established. 'No contact report? What the fuck is going on out there?' he asks Kev.

Kev springs into action as I look on. 'Hello Topaz Two Zero this is Topaz Zero Alpha, send sitrep over' He repeats the message. 'Hello Topaz Two Zero this is... before Kev can finish the stricken call sign answers up.

'Topaz Zero Alpha this is Topaz Two Zero, we have one disabled vehicle that has rolled into the canal, roger so far over?' 'Topaz Zero Alpha, Roger'

'Topaz Two Zero, there are multiple pax trapped inside and the canal is water logged. We have set up a security cordon and a rescue team are at the sight of the vehicle over'. Topaz Two Zero this is Topaz Zero Alpha, keep me updated and let me know if you need us to deploy QRF, send LOCSTAT, over'.

'Topaz Two Zero, Roger that. Out'. 'Fuck me' says Monty, adding that 'This is all we need.' He goes to warn off the QRF (Quick Reaction Force) just in case they need to push out. It's dark and the stricken call sign are in a precarious situation.

We all know that it's not just the water that poses a threat, but also the fact that our guys are pinned down in a position for any length of time. The Taliban attack when you are most vulnerable so the guys had to act fast. I start to worry about our guys drowning out there, our vehicles especially the ones that offer protection from small arms could prove difficult to escape from and the thought of being trapped in one as it fills with water doesn't conjure up a great picture.

Drowning being right up there on my list of how not to die, regardless of people saying that its peaceful after the initial struggle, unfortunately it's the struggle that you are actually awake for. The ops room waits for news and it's not long before we are updated again. 'Hello Topaz Zero Alpha this is Topaz Two Zero. All pax have been extracted from the vehicle which is now immobilised, seeking permission to deny the stricken vehicle over'. 'Topaz Zero Alpha ...Roger Wait Out'.

Getting permission to deny a vehicle - in other words to permanently disable it - must go through the chain of command back at Brigade HQ.

With no means on extracting the stricken vehicle the established procedure is to destroy it with high explosives and make sure that any sensitive equipment does not fall into enemy hands. All the while that we wait, we have injured soldiers on the ground pinned down to one location. Needless to say B Company are in for another long evening.

Getting permission for a vehicle denial from Brigade HQ is never easy. Some logistician telling my chain of command to exhaust all other avenues before high explosives are used. The boss loses patience and gets onto the net himself to Brigade. He advises that all avenues have been exhausted and that this a hostile AO, permission for the denial is required immediately over'. There is a long pause, everyone in the room desperate for the right outcome. In under a minute permission is granted. There is a reason why you become an Infantry Company Commander. Major Clark is decisive, his tone on the net almost demanding the answer that he eventually gets. His confident manner reassures us all that we are in more than capable hands. The stricken convoy is moving again and finally limps into the patrol base well past midnight. My medical team set about assessing our unexpected casualties. This time there is no blood or gore to patch up, only potential spinal problems and possible fractures.

Ensuring that there are no life or limb threatening injuries I decide to advise the boss that a casualty lift at first light is possible and no MERT is required straight away. This affords Major Clark some time as I explain that these men are no longer capable of fighting. The boss will always have the final say in the casevac of his men, as sometimes good medicine can mean bad tactics.

I advise him as his subject matter expert, he then weighs up the pros and cons and makes a decision. I have learned to always consider the tactical situation before coming to my own conclusion and this reassures Major Clark. 'Sgt T we will evacuate the guys at first light, have your team ready' 'Roger Sir, Thanks'.

I would get very frustrated when other soldiers would ask me why I was going through tactical courses. When I qualified as an Urban Operations Instructor. It wasn't so I could count up the 100 bruises I sustained. It wasn't to teach other medics how to clear houses or villages. It was to understand potential casualty choke points, learning how an infantry company operates in a built up area, teaching junior medics how to best use difficult built up terrain to evacuate casualties and most of all how best not to become a burden to the infantry company that you supported. The days of conventional warfare are over and the Taliban have shown that they do not discriminate.

Any tactical course that enables me to understand the ramifications of the decisions that I make are welcome albeit tough at times. Before I hit my roll mat I finish the wish list that I started earlier in the day. There is talk of a helicopter re-supply and I had to get my head around what we needed if our casualty rate continued as it had started. I eventually hit my pit space at well gone 2 am.

My medics are out on the ground tomorrow so they need their rest. I am beat, but no sooner had I shut my eyes I hear the dreaded words of 'Stand To' 'What the fuck?' I groan. I look at Kev and just want to close my eyes again, but no. Like a fucking robot I get up put my body armour on then my helmet chin strap secure before I proceed to the medical room where I find the rest of my team. I am relieved to see that everyone looks like shite, same detail as yesterday.

Call to prayer is my call to the yellow multi-purpose Sharps container. Climbing into the back of the Snatch Land Rover I think about the non-politically correct Army poster that says 'No one likes a dirty Snatch'. Of all the things to say, this lifts my mood as I go about my personal chores.

News from the ops room says that wheels will be up from Bastion shortly so my team begin to tend the wounded, we have four sorry looking soldiers and a night in the cold has not helped their now rigid bodies.

Mild whiplash would probably be feeling like a broken neck this morning. We have no means of spinal control and as with everything grunts crack on unless they are physically unable to do so. We walk our wounded out under the watchful eye of Sgt Major Davey's team who have already secured the routes and landing site. The helicopter lands, a Sea King, and is on the ground no longer than 20 seconds.

As it rises its creates a spiral of dust, this time I had positioned myself so I didn't get blasted by the debris on the floor. Back in the Patrol Base preparations for a foot patrol are under way, Sean will deploy out this morning. Jen is getting some well-earned rest after her late night, myself and Abbie settle in to the ops room on standby should we be required to deploy out with the QRF.

I barely know what day it is and doze off in my bed space. I am woken up by Abbie on account of my snoring, normally I would be a little embarrassed at snoring but in this arena I couldn't care less. I could probably count six hours sleep in the last three days and that's stimulant free, I was literally running on empty. I could feel myself getting annoyed so I moved next door to the medical post to chat with Davey, it wasn't long before I was sprawled out on the stretcher snoring again.

Three hours later Davey wakes me up in hysterics, he jokes that I had just managed to sleep through a small arms attack on the base. Feeling refreshed again I get the brews on. I knew that I had to get into routine and rest is a major part of that. Everyone in the base was struggling with lack of sleep.

CHAPTER THREE

The Shooting Season

We have been briefed that more Taliban fighters are heading for Nad-e Ali from across southern Helmand and it is clear that insurgent activity on the ground has increased. These fresh Jihadists appear happy to battle it out with our neighbours, A Company, 5 Scots, who are holding Garmsir. It appears the insurgents then skirt around Marjah, stopping only for replenishment of food, water and ammunition before hitting us. If they achieve victory here the entire mission will fail.

Nad-e Ali sits too close to the provincial capital Lashkar Gah. Defeat would be a strategic disaster. The so called 'Shooting Season' has reached its high point. Our patrol base is isolated; it's easy to feel that Brigade Headquarters has forgotten about us. The threat of one of our helicopters being shot down is now so high that aircraft will only fly into us at night or at dawn. Once on the ground, the pilots do not hang around they drop or collect and are quickly off to reduce the chance of an attack.

The aviation planners try to make sure that the Chinooks do not establish patterns of flying. It's now obvious to any observer that when helicopters do come to the base it is at night or first thing in the morning. So a pattern has been established. Most of the older cynical soldiers have deduced that we were here for one key reason, to make sure the Taliban don't mount any form of attack on the Kajaki operation. We are not even a full Company and our casualty rate is un-sustainable. The Kajaki mission has been on the cards for months, we all know that is the main focus and 'big picture' for the Brigade, but we knew very little about the operation. The aim is the delivery of a third turbine, which will allow Chinese contractors to get the hydro-electric dam to work at full capacity and provide power to Kandahar and southern Afghanistan. If successful the operation will be the catalyst to kick start future development. It will also make history as the Coalition's biggest operation in the south.

Every commander likes to throw around 'the big picture' comment, but we have heard too much about the big picture. At the end of the day when you are stinking, piss wet through with sweat, walking around in seven week old pants, eating shite scoff and constipated from that shite scoff no-one wants to hear the words 'bigger picture'.

All the big picture was doing was starting to piss people off. Every man understands that there is a task to do so let's just leave it at that. Save the bollocks part of the mission for dinner parties. Men on the ground want to know two things, when are they going home? And when are their replacements turning up? So just when we thought that we were all alone in Nad-e Ali, it was a relief to find that another friendly unit is in our area. These soldiers were reservists whose role in Helmand was as part of the Police Mentoring Team or PMT. The title PMT and the potential humorous implication of the Pre Menstrual Tension unit raised too many smiles and comments so we dubbed them 'the Throatcutters' which sounded much more hardcore.

I am sure there will be a T-shirt available in short time emblazoned with 'the Throatcutters', maybe on the back of a North Face jacket. They had been operating across Helmand for two months, living with and mentoring the Afghan Police who have been getting attacked on a daily basis. Our base is under attack again once more and the gun position on the roof appears to have been the target. Scotty Pew and his men must have put a dent in enemy numbers, seemingly their mission was to now take out that gun position. The sandbag reinforced walls are doing their job in holding the insurgents' high velocity rounds at bay.

Although the task of rebuilding the wall daily is dangerous and back breaking, the benefits far out- weigh the negatives, so Scotty works on a shift system for the lads on the roof. They sleep up there as movement up and down leaves them wide open to enemy fire. Pot marks in the wall underneath the position show how hard the enemy want to take them out.

We quickly receive news that the Afghan Police Station and the school that we spent our first night in has been hit hard and initial reports over the net confirm three casualties. The Afghan Police were instructed to bring their wounded to our location. Their main compound has taken a couple of direct hits from rocket propelled grenades. Only two nights ago we stayed there, I am beginning to think that lady luck gets to play a big part in all of this. Skill alone does not decide who lives or who dies. Time and place both play a huge part in whose day is ending badly, many serving in the military adopt the attitude that if it's your time then it's your time, you could be the best soldier in the world but a stray round of 7.62 or In-Direct Fire (IDF) may just have your name on it. It's not a pleasant thought, but how else would we do what we do? I have one medic out on the ground so there are three of us left. We prepare our makeshift aid post for the incoming casualties. Every man is busy.

I notice the smell coming from underneath my body armour. It's not good. There is little water and a good scrub is not possible. Most soldiers don't mind their own smell. There is definitely a time and a place for girl stuff; I do that when I go home. I leave the baggy, earth tone clothing in Afghanistan and go back to being normal for a bit.

I couldn't imagine anything worse than worrying about looking attractive out here, or periods for that matter. Female soldiers are encouraged to have a depo-provera injection. It's a form of contraception that stops periods altogether. Not designed for long term use it is a life saver for woman serving overseas. It's not my favourite subject; I recall when I was younger and starting that god-awful thing that women the world over go through. I remember asking my mum if I could have a hysterectomy as this monthly 'thing' was interfering with my daily activities. Being the mother of five children she looked at me through her smiling Irish eyes and told me that I might need it one day. Thanks Mum! What does become apparent though is just how fragrant you really are when you start to smell yourself.

We wait for the Afghan National Police casualties to turn up. When they arrive they are brought straight in. Yet again they don't appear concerned that they are receiving treatment from female soldiers.

I realise then that medicine is the only area in which a woman could probably get away with interacting with the men of this country. Afghan men run society, the women only speak when told to and the males make all the decisions. Women are regarded as second class citizens.

The injured Afghan men do not want to shake our hands and we don't force it. The sooner we accept the cultural differences, the better we will fair. Medicine breaks down barriers the world over and as yet is the only thing to do so. After a quick medical assessment I leave Abbie and Sean to crack on and initiate the Nine Liner call to Headquarters. It's a luxury to have such high calibre medics in my team they make my job appear easy at times. Kev relays all of the information that I have given him to Brigade.

He occasionally likes to add his own spin on messages, so Major Clark snaps at him to relay information word for word. Kev looks at me with a naughty child-like grin. No one is immune to getting gripped by the boss and rightly so. If you have never been gripped by your commander then you you are doing something wrong. I return to the medical room to check in on my guys. After quick medical interventions the three casualties are stable enough to be evacuated. The Afghan Police appear to have got off lightly.

Another crisis has been avoided. Surely that is our lot today. I am starting to lose count of the casualties that we have treated. We make the now familiar trip out to the helicopter site. The Afghan soldiers on the base help to carry the stretchers onto the Chinook. They haven't been trained in any type of helicopter handling so giving a lesson with real casualties turned into a scene out of the American cartoon series 'Ren and Stimpy'. I have come to believe that if you see it in a Tom and Jerry cartoon then you will most definitely see it in Afghanistan and more than likely it will be Afghan soldiers. They have no sense of danger at all and on the battlefield their 'bravery' is often out of all proportion to their sense of fear.

In 2006 when the first British troops arrived in the area men from the Royal Irish Regiment were assigned to mentor Afghan Army units. After a fierce battle in Garmsir the Royal Irish reported that the Afghans were 'mental' and refused to take cover in a contact, running straight towards the enemy.

Then when their commander was shot dead they stopped fighting and prepared to mourn his death. They had to be 'fired up' by Royal Irish soldiers to make sure they got back into the battle. It quickly became apparent that the Afghan's tactical awareness was very different to that of UK forces.

We return to the medical room and quickly replenish any kit that was used on the Afghan casualties. Once again I retreat to the peace and quiet of the medical room to catch a couple of hours sleep. The noise from the radio next door ensures that it is never a deep one. It's not long before I learn that Scotty's boys are in trouble. I am up quickly and straight into the ops room. They are just over a kilometre away and they have been heavily ambushed. They are in vehicles and through the haze of battle it emerges that one of the vehicles has been cut off. My heart is literally pushing at my throat. The thought of any of our boys being captured makes me feel physically sick. The boss is beside himself.

Panicked voices over the radio net do not paint a good picture. Monty is already mounted up ready to provide QRF to the stricken convoy. Its times like this when an experienced commander does not make a knee jerk reaction. Monty is chomping at the bit to get to his friend Scotty, but the boss knows that it will add to our woes and could potentially have a catastrophic result until we know exactly what the facts are. This is the one time that I really get to see a Commander at work. Major Clark is pacing up and down going through every possible scenario. He speaks calmly and direct. 'Monty stand your men to and await further orders' 'Roger that Sir' Monty replies.

In one motion he has eased Monty's tension by standing the Quick Reaction Force ready to move. Over the net Lt Barclay, their young Platoon Commander barely out of Sandhurst Military Academy (British Army Officer Training) runs through options of where the vehicle may have gone. He and Scotty start make a quick combat estimate – finding a workable plan. By now the boss has eyes on the area with the use of a video link from an Unmanned Aerial Vehicle (UAV) drone.

Barclay's estimate was uncomplicated and direct. He says 'So what? We are missing a vehicle and three of my men. Therefore? We are going back into the kill zone to get them'. Combat estimate complete!

Barclay selflessly decides to go back into the kill zone to try to find his men. His platoon, his soldiers, do not question his decision for a second, they are just as desperate to find their missing comrades. The ops room is silent. We sit and stare at each other and then stare at the radio. Even if Mr Barclay does find them, the Taliban may have got to them first. It doesn't take long to kill someone. During our pre-deployment training back in the UK it was made clear to us that if the Taliban capture you, it is likely to be game over. They will execute you and possibly film it for distribution on the internet. Fifteen minutes pass without news. It is becoming unbearable.

Mr Barclay is still searching and there is no sign of the missing WMIK. Another fifteen minutes and there is a burst across the radio 'Man down ! Man down!'

My heart races again as silence follows. What the hell is going on out there? I start thinking of the implications of our guys being captured. I do well to stop this speculative train of thought and concentrate on what's actually happening.

More information is coming through and suddenly relief - the boss's face says it all. They have found the missing soldiers, but Mr Barclay has been shot in the thigh during their rescue. He would later receive the Military Cross for his actions. Every Jock is waiting for news. I am anxious to get hold of the casualties as time is precious when soldiers are bleeding. The platoon break contact and head back to the base. Three soldiers have been injured and are preparing to be evacuated. The Platoon Commander's driver LCpl Vin la Roux has bilateral injuries to his ears after a close encounter with an RPG. Scotty has fractured his hand, and the young officer Mr Barclay has a gunshot wound to his upper thigh. Men were being injured on a daily basis so something had to give. The Afghan soldiers must now be forced to stand and fight with B Company. If they don't, Nad-e Ali will fall to the Taliban and that cannot be allowed to happen.

Barclay and Scotty are reluctant to go. Their departure is a blow to the company. They are the backbone of their platoon and Barclay is just starting on his career. For him this is what he has spent the last 18 months training for. I remind him that he has been shot. Between them they saved the lives of three soldiers. I can only imagine what that ambush was like. I could probably triple my own feelings of anxiety.

Just then trouble magnet Duffy tells me of his success with a 66 mm rocket. 'A direct hit, Channy, happy days mucker' was echoed throughout the base. He was happy that he had got some payback for his platoon.

Corporal Gaz Wallace was the vehicle commander who had been cut off with two others. Gaz was quiet and clearly needed a bit of space to take in what had happened. I will catch up with him if he needs me. The helicopter casualty evacuation goes off without incident. Later that evening the banter starts flying around the base with taunts about what might have happened if they had been taken prisoner. Jokes about orange boiler suits and getting bummed by the Taliban are rife. With the Jocks the insults are never far away and a good indicator to me that morale is still ok. In fact, the more inappropriate the better! This is the way that these soldiers dealt with the emotional trauma of it all.

If it didn't kill you then it was definitely worth laughing about.

The news that more soldiers are heading our way is welcomed. We have already heard about the Police Mentoring Team, now a special training unit called the OMLT (Operational Mentor and Liaison Team) will join us. The OMLT is a small six man training team, they will hopefully give direction to our Afghan soldiers and help shape them up. They have deployed from a much bigger UK training formation ,based near Bastion. They don't have a medic, so I will loan them one of ours. I choose Sean for the task as it's a small team of six men working closely with the Afghans.

While the Afghans accept our help medically in the base, I do not wish to push my luck by sending a female to live with and support them. Our numbers are falling fast so the arrival of the OMLT would give us a much needed uplift both in morale and numbers, even if they are small in number.

Monty is now the sole Platoon Sergeant and faces a lot of responsibility. He does have Cpl James Henderson as his second in command and Hendy from Wishaw is more than capable of holding the platoon together. Monty has Davey on hand for advice and I will be here to support him medically. He would just have to wait for a platoon commander.

Infantry soldiers are trained to step up if needed and take command, the obvious reason being if their commander is killed or wounded. Monty is a strong SNCO, he looks older than his years and commands respect. His men love him and my medics feel safe with him.

He is your typical Scotsman. Likes a drink and smokes as many cigarettes as the day will allow. He is a soldier that I would learn a great deal from. My Mum is Irish born and was raised in Glasgow, so I have no problems in getting heavily involved in the Jock banter. 'Shut it ya wee fanny' is a phrase that Ferris often receives. He is a comical young Jock who taunts all of the junior medics. He is, without realising it, the soldier's morale booster and is always looking for an opening to act up. I knew Ferris from my days as a depot instructor. He was a young recruit when our paths first crossed.

He was the same then as he is now…a pest! He had character and at times, that goes a very long way and he is a very popular member of B Company. I shake my head and laugh when I see that his very white arse is hanging out of a large hole in the back of his combats. Worse still he makes no attempt to cover it. I settle down into my bed space and dig out my iPod and engross myself in the solace of some of my favorite tunes. I select a top 25 and this would see me through the rest of my tour.

My iPod would turn out to be my one saving grace during these testing times. I lying in the dark between Jenny and Abbie and think about my brother, David. He was killed when I was on exercise in Cyprus. I keep a small picture of him in the inner sleeve of my body armour. It's always there and very important to me. Along with a set of Rosary beads. A friend of Dave's gave them to me to put in his casket. I didn't have the heart to tell her that the casket was closed, so I kept them with me. They had seen me through some rough times during my tours of Iraq in 2003 and Helmand in 2006. They were with me now, so if they get me home after this then they will stay with me forever. Losing Dave was the worst thing that ever happened to me.

The thought of losing blokes tonight reminded me of him. I know that if I were to die out here my one consolation would be that I would see him again. It's not long before I am up and running around in my body armour and helmet again. These moments are random but I suppose they happen to us all.

The Taliban let rip with another onslaught. Every attack is getting a little too close for comfort. Their Indirect Fire or IDF may not be as accurate as they would like, but we all know that it only takes one lucky shot and someone's day would be ending badly. Not today though.

I know that every man out here has their own story to tell so I dust myself off and move on safe in the knowledge that my brother will be watching over me from somewhere. I tally up the casualties and try to remember who was injured and when. My body and mind alike are fatigued. Lack of sleep is starting to take its toll. I gather the medical team and make sure that they are okay. I may be in a command position but these are my guys and their safety is always my concern. We would become great friends during our time in Nad-e Ali. Me and my medics are involved with every attack whether inside or outside of the base. We rely heavily on each other to get things right.

I think back to the summer 2006 when I deployed here with the 3rd Battalion The Parachute Regiment. I never fully understood what it meant to be under siege when the paras spoke about the battle for Sangin. Now Nad-e Ali was turning into our Sangin, you had to be here to understand it. The true lay of the land was known only by the enemy, this was their backyard and they knew every inch of it. When most units deploy into a base such as Nad-e Ali they are supported by a small artillery unit, as well as an Engineer squadron building up defensive walls. We had nothing, unless things got really bad and then the Apache would be assigned to our Joint Tactical Air Controller (JTAC).

In fact even the rations we have are quite literally being rationed. The young men fighting are ageing well beyond their years. But we do have lots of intelligence support and are able to use technology to support our understanding of the Taliban's intentions and plans. It is very clear that we have been sent to hold the line against the enemy in Nad-e Ali and make sure they do not spark any level of attack that forces the Commander to pull more troops away from the turbine move and compromise that operation.

Another night passes. Activity in the base starts early, everyone is up as Monty prepares to take his platoon out. As soon as any patrol leaves the base everyone goes on to a heightened state. The thought of the base being overrun is always a constant threat. One of our guys has already killed at least 20 fighters, he doesn't shout about it but his success is well known across the company. The Apache gunships who have been regular visitors have torn up many more.

The Taliban's battlefield replacement plan seems to be working well, no matter how many we kill they are able to replace them and fast. We are lucky if we have two full platoons left. Monty's platoon are out for less than half an hour before they are hit. I can hear Monty over the net. I hear his fire control orders clearly, almost like he is standing in the same room.

He is calling for Close Air Support (CAS) and our JTAC, the modern day forward air controller, wastes no time in getting it to him. It sounds like some of the lads have been pinned down on the wrong side of a ditch. It's not like the films where you can run along tracks and dodge rounds. If you are up and running then the likely-hood of you getting shot generally multiplies. Cpl Tam Rankine, one of the more experienced section commanders knows that the soldiers are in trouble. He sprints across the open ground to try and give them more fire power. He gets shot in the hand during the rescue. He got off lightly and knows it. He would later be written up for his bravery.

After accurate use of the 66 mm, the men manage to make good the ground that they have lost. Jenny treats Tam when she can, and calls in the casualty over the net. The guys are in the middle of a firefight so it's down to me and Davey to go out and retrieve our wounded. My man Duffy has also been injured and it doesn't surprise me that he is in the thick of it.

The 'Throatcutters' are operating elsewhere, but provide our Quick Reaction Force or QRF. We set off in three vehicles. I'm top cover for Davey and have a 66 mm rocket beside me. It suddenly dawns on me as I check the 66 mm as to how lucky I am. My path in life could have resulted very differently.

I am in a world that few men or women have the chance to experience. All medics that hail from 16 Brigade who are attached to Infantry companies are given an insight into all the weapon systems that the company employs.

The Taliban does not discriminate in fact they will pay a tidy bounty for the death of a British military female. In Basra insurgents made it known that they would pay their fighters $100,000 for a captured white, blonde British soldier. I tick all the boxes. The Taliban will attack anyone and when it kicks off everyone can look forward to getting a slice, this is not a conventional conflict with prisoner of war camps, where the Geneva convention means something, it doesn't. The waving of a red cross doesn't cut it out here. These lads are fighting hard and I would feel ashamed if I couldn't offer a safe haven to them if they get injured. I would protect my casualties by any means necessary.

We head to where the fire is coming from. Driving into contact is no joke. All I can think about is that hideous heavy weapon that the Taliban have been smashing the base with. A direct hit from the Dshk would cut me in half. I look in the distance through the sight on top of my SA80, it is called a SUSAT (Sight Unit Small Arms Trilux). I spot Jenny running with her casualties. The noise is deafening! Davey sees Jen and makes a hasty stop.

We get out of the vehicles and take her casualties. I watch Jen go running back to the platoon sergeants group and with Monty she just cracks on. I like the fact that you can't tell her apart from the others. The running we did around the landing site in our Osprey body armour back at Lash has paid off handsomely.

I get my casualties in the wagon and we head back to the base. Once there I examine Tam and Duffy. As per usual Duffy finds something to joke about laughing at the fact that they were; 'Shitting themselves when they were cut off'. I am relieved that Duffy is okay. Losing someone so young with such character doesn't bear thinking about and I have grown quite fond of his once annoying habits. The boss needs a casualty report and fast. I assess these guys as Cat C's which means we have four hours to play with. The fire fight hasn't finished so at the moment the chance of more casualties is very high. One thing that I am struggling with today is the Afghan heat. It's stifling. I drink two bottles of water in one go almost making myself sick. The platoon eventually breaks contact and are heading back in. I discover that Kev has already sent the Nine Liner declaring that we have a Cat B casualty. I am angered with the lack of communication. This has become common place on the battlefield and sometimes medics are too scared to speak out.

I am concerned that this is the wrong decision and I approach Major Clark . We get on well so I don't want any type of confrontation nor I don't want to make a situation out of nothing.

I explain that the guy's injuries do not require such a high priority and we should change the Cat back down to a C. He says that the helicopter and MERT team may not come if we put Tam as a Cat C. I explain that there may be more needy casualties up country and that if we start over-categorising patients then Brigade will question all of our Nine Liners.

I am anxious and want him to agree with me. I understand what he is feeling and his actions are always for the benefit of his men. I just want him to trust me and know that I need his support on this. I explain that I can send a casualty update over the net ensuring that they know that four hours is our cut-off and that if it's any longer then the damage to Tam's hand becomes permanent. The MERT commander can then make an informed decision. The boss agrees and allows me to downgrade Tam and Duffy. No one is at fault here. Kev heard that Tam had a gunshot wound and automatically thought he was a Cat B. I am relieved that this has been resolved and if anything has cemented my relationship with the boss. I set about preparing Tam and Duffy for evacuation.

The rest of Monty's platoon get back and Davey meets them at the gate with water and re-hydration satchets of Lucozade. This would become a routine chore. Whoever was out would receive water and a Lucozade satchet at the front gate when they got back in. It was a good way to check the morale of the men and also check their physical well-being.

Just by looking at a soldier's face and body language can tell you a great deal. It was a far better system than allowing soldiers to quietly go off and administer themselves. If heat illness goes untreated it becomes deadly. A few of the lads come into the medical post to check in on Duffy and Tam. We receive word that the MERT team and their Chinook are preparing to launch from Bastion to pick up our casualties. This is welcome news. The boss and Captain Wood, our second in command, reassure me that we made the right call with Tam. I am relieved that the MERT team took the decision to come.

We all put our faith in the system and this time it has worked. Sometimes there may be a casualty far more desperate than us for the Casevac. I take a moment to think about my friends up north manning the Forward Operating Bases. Our Brigade has taken the fight to the Taliban and in doing so has taken a lot of casualties during the tour.

Our medical regiment is close knit and any bad news involving a medic would have a devastating effect on us all. The MERT call prompts us to push ourselves out towards the front gate. We get our casualties in the shade and sit and wait. I contemplate taking them back up to the aid post as I am informed that the MERT helicopter has yet to launch. I check in with Kev at the ops room who tells me that the helicopter is finally 'wheels up' at Bastion and on the way.

A few of the lads have joined our group to bid farewell to their muckers. I see that Stevie Howie is in the group, he is a tough lad brought up on a rough council scheme in Glasgow. He has a strong character and manages to look as fresh as a daisy even though he has just endured a two hour contact during the hottest part of the day.

All of a sudden there is a feeling of panic and danger around us. An Afghan soldier has narrowly missed me and my casualties with his Ford Ranger pickup truck, 'Jesus fuckin Christ' someone screams. The driver wasn't even a metre away and we were literally inches from the wheels. The idiot didn't see what he had done and continued to drive on leaving us in a heap on the ground. Stevie jumps up and goes nuts, he brings his weapon to bear at the Afghan and starts yelling 'You stupit fuckin prick! You stupit fuckin prick!'

Everyone in the group adds their ten pence worth. Our guys are taking the brunt of the casualties out on the ground, and this fool nearly mows down about six of us in the patrol base. The Afghan soldiers have been refusing to go out of the base so this heightens an already tense situation. We manage to calm Stevie down and I am relieved that I can hear the sound of a Chinook in the distance. I tell the guys that we need to push out. Stevie was justified in his actions and showed tremendous restraint at not losing it completely. It would be naive to judge his actions, he has just spent the last two hours fighting off the Taliban.

When we get back I will speak with Major Clark, who will later speak to the Kandak commander. The ANA soldiers needed much guidance so the arrival of the OMLT couldn't come fast enough. We have been told they are on the way, but we have still not seen them. Duffy places his arm around my neck and shoulders as I help him hobble onto the ramp of the Chinook. Abbie does the same for Tam. As quick as the wheels are down they are off again. I receive a reassuring pat on the back from the door gunner on my way off. It caught me off guard and I then think does he know something that I don't? I guessed that we were here for the long haul, or at least until the Marines take over. Jesus, I thought, that was just shy of two months away!

CHAPTER FOUR

'Flashheart' Arrives

The base has settled down once more and everyone waits for the usual twilight attack. It comes like clockwork. We are under siege again random bursts of .50 cal from the Dhsk remind everyone that the Taliban are equipped with more than just their ability to lay IEDs. What they lack in skill and discipline is more than made up for in the will to keep going. When you choose to take on an insurgency brainwashed and under the influence of the Opium poppy it's no surprise that they never tire of being slotted. As one falls, another is on hand to pick up his AK47. On the plus side morale amongst our group is still good. Banter and insults flying around gives a useful indication as to level of spirit amongst the blokes. The banter has moved to my music, which has come under scrutiny as the Counting Crows play through a small speaker that I had stashed in my day sack. Certain items make life bearable in times of strife so along with my yellow sharps container the speaker was a must for my own sanity and morale.

I went to war in Kosovo with Van Morrison, Paul Simon smashed Sierra Leone, Hootie and the Blowfish in Iraq and Snow Patrol here in 2006. I have an album that gets played to death on every deployment. The tracks ping memories that I hadn't thought of since the day the incident happened.

Dylan, The Stones, Creedance Clearwater Revival (CCR) are basics on all tours. Music is an important part of my life and every experience good or bad has a sound track. It's the way I come to understand things or at least put them into perspective. If I could have chosen a path for myself it would have been singer or songwriter, perhaps both. I used to write lyrics and poetry as a child, the poetry grew darker through my teenage years I put much of that down to the haze that engulfed me through my abuse of Cannabis. The writing stopped in my early twenties as did the Cannabis use when I realised that I didn't sound much like Sheryl Crow. I opted to join the Army as a Combat Medic instead. Sitting on my stretcher in the Company Aid Post in my blood-stained combats I knew that I had made the right decision.

Today, the Crows are the focus of much discussion, it's not long before I am also pinged to marry the interpreter that I spooned with to keep warm on night one. Kev says : 'Puttin out on the first date eh mucker?' which has everyone rolling about with laughter.

'Nice one Kev...ya prick!' Kev and I had a brother and sister relationship down to a tee. Laughing I roll over on my stretcher and turn my back on Monty and against my better judgement my speaker. I barely close my eyes when all of a sudden Michael Buble starts bellowing out of my speaker. 'What the fuck is this?' I shout out. Monty laughs before grabbing my speaker ensuring that it's out of reach of me. He tries in vain to defend his own collection of Buble Swing. 'Nice! Just the type of banging tunes you expect from a Scottish warrior eh Monty, or shall I call you Margot from now on?' Within minutes the Crows are back on, already in hard cover we continue to sprawl out on the stretchers and roll mats on the floor. We laugh and joke about the different events that have taken place over the past few months. Without warning our banter is interrupted.

We frezze for a second, as rounds start winging their way in through the blacked out windows of the room we are in. A round ricochets off the old blackboard and bounces around the floor in front of me. Monty starts laughing. It's more of a nervous 'what the fuck is that' laugh.

We all pause for a second and wonder where else to take cover, we were already in hard cover and already on the ground. I start laughing at Davey's quick reactions. He was like a stunned gazelle!

We roll about like children happy in the knowledge that the rounds haven't hit anyone. This was getting outrageous and I guess we were high on adrenaline. It's strange, you get so used to rounds bouncing around that it doesn't bother you like it should. The barrage peters out and I start what would become a daily ritual. I roll and smoke a cigarette. It almost signifies the end of a day and it gives me something to look forward to.

I certainly wasn't a huge smoker prior to this 'atmospherics' check on Nad-e Ali. I was a social smoker if at all. By now everyone is busy in their own routine. That means either eating, sleeping, fighting or bleeding. The 'rabbit in headlights' look has faded and the guys know the importance of rest and look forward to the peace that the night time brings. Myself and Davey start a daily walk round of all of our positions. It's to check on morale more than anything. Davey asks me to check in on Freddie McCabe, he is one of the young soldiers who had been cut off earlier today and Monty says he is not acting himself. Freddie 18, is not mouthing off and in this world that is a cause for concern. Monty thinks that he might be blaming himself for Tam getting shot. No one wants to be the bloke who needs help. But at his age, he is going through a lot more than his peer group at home. Just like Duffy he could have chosen a very different path in life.

Freddie is a young soldier who walks with the typical infantry swagger and has the attitude to match. He is a fan of hardcore rave music and cans of Red Bull, just like Duffy. I ask him for a quick chat. He is reluctant at first until I tell him that he can either talk to me or someone else back in Camp Bastion. This makes his decision easy and he can also blame me for forcing him to speak if the other Jocks give him abuse. I think these situations are easier for a female sometimes.

Men worry that they will be judged if they show any weakness. When you are 18 and you are fighting this hard, with your friends falling beside you. Sometimes you need that cup of tea and a chat. Yet again I begin morphing into my Nan with the whole cup of tea thing. 'Right so you have had both your legs blown off and could potentially lose a ballsack. How about a nice cup of tea and a digestive biscuit?' Chuckling I explain the scenario to Freddie, he says that he wouldn't mind the conversation, if the tea was replaced with a Red Bull.

He gestures for us to sit down on a makeshift bench. Freddie doesn't need me to patronize him so rather than beat around the bush I just ask him straight up what happened and let him do the talking. He relays all of the details describing of the incident and the feeling of panic at being cut off from his platoon, which I am sure everyone would feel.

I remind him of the events of the WMIK getting cut off and explain that it's normal to be freaked out. I make light of the situation and joke with him that he may have shit his pants just as Duffy had said. he had done. I added that unfortunately I had no spare to give him!

He laughs and tells me 'No fucking way'. We talk for about ten minutes and I explain that people are worried for him. I reassure him that all of us are in new territory here regardless of how many years we have served. I tell him that fear is healthy and that's what probably kept him alive. I add that all of my tours could be described as relatively quiet compared to this one. He laughs when I remind him about Duffy. Even though Duffy has been evacuated he still manages to bring happiness to the company in his own special needs way. I laugh at the thought of him being back in Lashkar Gah, annoying people again with his happy hardcore banter. Monty was right though he was worried for Tam and Duffy. I reassure him that they will both be fine. Ferris walks past us as we are talking and tells Freddy to, 'Shut the fuck up!' Freddie replies 'Get te fuck ya wee ball bag'. This alone tells me that Freddie will bounce back easily. In situations like this I think the best therapy is from the people that you share the experience with. They won't allow you to dwell too much on it and you repay the compliment by just cracking on.

I know that many of the remaining soldiers will be thinking about the days or weeks ahead and when will it be their turn to get whacked, they are seeing their mates evacuated on the MERT helo to Bastion. The number of soldiers here is slowly going down. It is not a good feeling. It is though something we all share and try to ignore. When we get back to the UK we will talk to other soldiers about it. Often when soldiers go home and people say 'we just want them to open up and talk to us about what they have been through', the truth is we just don't want to. It's not something that you can be a part of, as you weren't there.

I have often tried to describe certain situations at home to friends. When they unintentionally start to look bored, I proceed to talk to my glass of Jack Daniels and Coke and enjoy its response far more. That's just the way it is.

There is eventually some good news from Lash. We are getting a re-supply tonight along with a team of instructors for the Afghan National Army. Fantastic news, they should have been here days ago, but they have been delayed like so many things in this part of the world. Monty will also get a platoon commander. The new arrivals, the Operational Mentor and Liaison Team (OMLT), drawn mainly from the Royal Irish Regiment will work and live among the Afghans.

In my opinion this is another thankless task. We we know from hard experience that rogue Afghans have taken a gun to British troops several times.

The day passes without incident and everyone looks forward to the re-supply. I do a little personal administration, clean my weapon, wash my smalls and dust my feet with powder. I am looking forward to the introduction of some new rations as the same old ration pack food is killing me. I am desperate to taste something other than mashed up steak and vegetables served in the special Army foil packet.

I am conscious of the fact that my arse is also in danger of being on display to the general populous of the base. The thin material of my combats is wearing away and rapidly. They are covered in blood and grime and in desperate need of a wash.

Even the boss has commented on the state of them. 'It's official. Sgt Taylor has gone feral'. The boss announces over a non-existent loud speaker system. Everyone's kit is in turmoil. The medics back at Lash should hopefully have packed up some kit for the four of us out here, which will be sent down on the re-supply. I know that I can rely on them and for a moment I miss the banter back in the medical section. I wonder if they know what is going on out here. I am sure that they will have had their own casualties to worry about.

We had a fair few ourselves when we were back there. The atmosphere around the base is buzzing. The re-supply is probably the first bit of good news that we have received in the last six days. The Royal Irish team from the OMLT will take some of the pressure off the boss, especially when it comes to the handling of the Afghans. They will now have a full team to mentor them out on the ground, which will be a great help.

Looking after yourself and your team is a challenge in itself, but directing a patrol of Afghans, many of who seem to mince around with their safety catch off is a major concern, at least for me anyway. I ask Abbie to calculate our casualty figures while we adjust some of the kit in the medical room. She sounds surprised at what she finds. She shouts out 'Thirty, we have evacuated thirty casualties!'

Even now I struggle to remember them all. It's like the past six days have been a blur. I try to recap all of the injured and can't actually remember them. I look at the book ... evacuated 30 casualties in six days? It's not that I am bothered by that particular number. It's the fact that I realise that we are possibly here for the next two months. What on earth does the future hold? I have no doctor to rely on and our medical kit is minimal. I check the re-supply list that I have made and start thinking long term.

I just write down anything that comes to mind. Funnily enough the majority of it involves bleed kits. I'm not a fan of medics playing god. I like to evacuate serious bleeds quickly. I have no replacement blood to give and casualties are always going to be better off when they reach Bastion. It's not a time for me or my medics to start experimenting with our skills. Identifying the need for early surgery is a skill that we as a Brigade have mastered very well and use to great effect. Our drill is clear. Only make limb or life saving interventions and leave the rest to the surgeon's knife.

B Company and the Afghans are being hit hard. I have noticed one thing in myself and the others on day six. The wide eyed stares had disappeared. The soldiers of B Company were no longer bothered by the situation in which they had now found themselves. Even the last light attacks had become a bit of a circus.

If it took only six days to become hardened to the ferocity of this war, then how long would it take for these men to recover from the emotional scars that combat had inflicted on them? British troops had, along with the Americans sustained casualties and endured heavy fighting in both Afghanistan and Iraq. Where would we go next? From my point of view I can see that the psychological impact on our soldiers is yet to be measured.

I have read and learned from older colleagues that combat stress was high in Northern Ireland and many other conflicts. In Ulster at the height of the troubles the fear of being shot dead in a sniper attack created a huge psychological impact on young soldiers. The Iraq campaign delivered a new kind of fear of being captured and beheaded by insurgents.

These modern day conflicts are not like the battles of World War Two, which while themselves were mentally and physically draining, the soldiers knew that in the main, if captured they would be sent to a prisoner of war camp. Afghanistan and Iraq are barbaric. Here the Taliban will hang a pregnant mother and cut her open in the street if they think she has spoken to Coalition forces and British soldiers see that.

Post Traumatic Stress Disorder (PTSD) has been prevalent for many years among those that have served here. Military life has always encouraged a heavy drinking culture throughout the ranks and we, the British public, live in a society that is dominated by alcohol. This is all well and good in moderation. For men and woman coming home from conflict who may have experienced hardship or situations that have affected them mentally, the struggle to integrate back into normal life can be difficult and the problems often go unnoticed.

The more time that you spend in a uniform the more institutionalised you become. My family noticed changes in me and my lack of patience would sometimes cause me to act irrationally. I recall standing in line in a cobblers shop when the man in front of me seemed to take an age over what he wanted. He kept repeating himself time and time again. I could feel myself getting angry and before I could do anything I found myself gripping him for taking too long. The way I spoke to him was unacceptable, but at the time I didn't comprehend what I was saying. He looked taken aback. As I stormed out of the shop I felt embarrassed and wondered what had come over me.

I had strived to do well all of my life, but I had become over efficient at everything, almost robotic. I was obsessed with getting tasks done at warp speed or ensuring that I was direct and straight to the point about everything. My phone manner was borderline Jeremy Paxman. Rebuking sales advisors about my inefficient phone contract or beasting my banking phone service about unknown transactions. I was literally wearing myself out and worst still I was wearing my family out. I recognised quickly what I was doing and toned down my enthusiasm to three - quarter warp speed, I had always been motivated and that was part of my charm, so I couldn't put it all down to PTSD.

I just had to stop with the public berating of people. The shoe guy was lucky that tar and feathering was no longer acceptable. Cases of PTSD will simmer away until someone gets help or someone snaps.

I often relate to the film 'Falling Down' with Michael Douglas and can relate to just wanting to lose it sometimes. The way the UK has fallen into a quagmire of 'the haven for terrorists who seem to say and do what they like' does not help matters. When our fallen come home and are at risk from protest and disruption, or our soldiers are called murderers and child killers as they march through their home towns it angers me. I can see why and how someone will one day 'lose it', just like the guy in the film 'Falling Down', who snaps and goes on a killing spree.

Time draws close to the eagerly awaited re-supply. It's the back of midnight and the helicopter landing zone is secured and ready to receive. The Chinook lands and begins to drop off its load. One, two. three, four, five and six. I count the crates for Davey as they come off. The helicopter isn't down for long and takes off under the cover of darkness. A mouthful of dirt for me, mega. My teeth are sticking to my lips and unless I get to some water soon that is the way that they will stay. Davey calls for the All-Terrain Vehicle (ATV) and trailer to come forward.

Cpl Ham Mclaughlin is driving it, he is without a doubt the funniest bloke in the company. He has a dry sense of humour and even when he is pissed off he can still manage to make a joke of something. The fact that he was pissed off was enough to make me laugh. He was constantly fucking with people and their kit. If your chair was suddenly missing and you fell on your arse where your chair once sat, then you could be sure that he had something, or everything to do with it. Ham was spending most of his time between the wall and the roof. He was another soldier suffering from a 'ten years older' makeover. He would constantly ask me what I knew about when we were getting out of here. Ham had been in Marjah with me and Kev so we were all a tight-knit group.

Everyone mucked in to help off-load the pallets while he shuttles back and forth into the base. I notice that there are some clean looking soldiers helping off-load the eagerly awaited cargo. Great, I thought, this must be the overdue OMLT. I immediately hear the unmistakable and irritating tones of what can only be an officer. Worse still he sounds like a Guards officer. The officers of 5 Scots were rough around the edges and that was exactly what this war needed. No pomp and ceremony, just meat eating warriors with a lot of attitude.

Proper introductions with the new guys would have to wait until tomorrow, I was in no mood to speak to anyone. It was late and I wanted to get back to my roll mat as quickly as I could. The boss had declared a no-patrol day tomorrow so everyone can take a well earned rest. I settle down to another restless night's sleep and it is not long before the bright sunshine initiates another early start. My unkempt hair is slowly turning into dreadlocks. I am very aware of the fact that I am really starting to smell. The OMLT look far too clean compared to the rest of us. Rest assured though it wouldn't be long until they were just as dishevelled.

These guys had already been involved in heavy fighting up north. I wondered how they would compare their past experience to life in Nad-e Ali. The arrival of the OMLT reminded me of the Royal Irish soldiers that served with the Brigade in the summer of 2006. I think about Spence, a Royal Irish Colour Sergeant, who had taught me a hard lesson during my tactics course down at the Infantry Training Centre in Wales. He had been injured in the Sangin Valley on a tour in 2006. I had learnt a great deal from him and found that he had given me an unexpected appreciation of what we call the ferocious - or the teeth arms. In in one particular training attack I was appointed the Number Two on the GPMG.

This meant that I was part of a two man gun team and would assist the gunner in carrying extra ammo. Initially I thought that I had a much easier task than going forward as one of the assaulting section. I recall my own smugness at the role that I had been given. I could just plonk myself into a fire support position until the enemy position had been cleared. How hard could that be? How wrong I was. It was only a matter of time before I realised that no one gets an easy job when it comes to fighting. The whole Platoon had already endured a long Tactical Advance to Battle (TAB) everyone was hanging out, (physically exhausted). When we came under effective enemy fire the Platoon advanced and began to close with the enemy. Gun teams began to move into positions including me and my gunner.

CSgt Spence decided to prematurely kill off my gunner, which left me carrying the heavy machine gun, my own weapon and all the machine guns rounds, or link as they are known, that we had been carried between us. 'Not so easy any more eh Sgt Taylor?' shouted Spence. What a dick I thought. Shuffling along before falling heavily into a fire support position as the instructors tried hard not to laugh as they watched me. Obviously I pretended that I was fine and dug deep to try not to show any signs of pain as my body smashed against rocks that were almost too well placed.

Feeling like both of my lungs were collapsing I continued to engage the enemy position. Only when the Re-Org , a term to pause and replenish ammo and await the next order, was called at the end of the assault did I wish that I was part of the assaulting section or that the exercise would end. Any plausible excuse that did not involve me having to run from my position to the enemy position would have been welcome. It was one of the hardest things that I had ever done. The sheer weight of all of my kit made me vomit a little down the front of my smock. Why hadn't I tried harder to expend fire ammunition?

During that tactics course I had a little taste of what an Infantry soldier does. I would be happy not to taste it again. Any soldier who has spent any amount of time in the Brecon Beacons of Wales will appreciate how hard the infantry get it. That's why most of them have a bit of an attitude. I would too if I had to go through junior and senior command courses down there.

As we sat talking Davey was relieved to find that there was a Sgt Major in the OMLT group. Someone to share his woes with and to act as his number two for any outgoing 51 mm mortar missions. Sgt Maj Tony Mason was quite a character. He had the luck of the Irish and this would see him and his crew through some rough times.

Monty's new platoon commander arrives in the shape of Second Lieutenant Du Boulay. He is straight out of Sandhurst and has not long arrived in country. I was unsure how a brand new officer would cope out here, even Mr Barclay had gathered some experience during the early months of the tour. Du Boulay would turn out to alleviate any doubts about his ability; in fact he would probably become one of the best officers that I have had the pleasure to serve with and would later receive a Mention in Dispatches for his courage and leadership under fire.

I finally get eyes on the guy with the irritating voice from the night before. It was no surprise that he resembled a character straight out of Blackadder. Ham McLaughlin came straight into the ops room and asked 'Who the fuck is that? Is he Flashheart from Blackadder?'. Jesus Christ I thought. He was tall with floppy blonde hair and a little awkward in his own skin. His attempts to make friends and influence people failed miserably, he carried the image of Flashheart, the World War One flying ace in the BBC comedy series. He was a snob and I think that even some of the officers were slightly embarrassed by his antics. He would be regularly reassured in no uncertain terms as to where he fell in the chain of command. But he did add to the team and that was important.

I think it's always good to have your share of every type of personality just to keep things interesting. He also bought with him some morale in the shape of his red iPod. The blokes borrowed it not on account that he had great taste in music. The red iPod was well stocked with a variety of entertainment. Anyway with Flashheart leading the Kandak into battle this was all about to get a little more interesting.

The boss's plan for a no-patrol day is welcome and relaxing. We get stuck into the medical room and unload the medical re-supply that has arrived. Weapons are cleaned and the lads are taking full advantage of getting some extra sleep. Everyone struggles to sleep in the heat of the day so sometimes just lying in your own sweat is better than nothing at all.

We are not let down when it comes to last light as the Taliban give their usual show of force. The only difference today is the introduction of the PK, a Russian designed 7.62 mm machine gun with an effective range of 1,000 meters. It's the Taliban equivalent of our own General Purpose Machine Gun. I imagine a Taliban soldier eating his scoff and just firing random bursts in our direction thankfully not accurately! We are sat in the ops room and the discussion turns to the important task of naming the Patrol Base, its something that all units do.

After about 40 minutes of banter it's no surprise that it is named Argyll on account of the soldiers defending it. I smile to myself and reveal the regiment's connection to my local football team, Plymouth Argyle. The name 'Argyle' is derived from the Argyll and Sutherland Highlanders who were stationed in Plymouth and won the Army Cup. At the turn of the century, Mr Howard Grose and Mr Pethybridge wanted to pursue their interest in football and it was suggested that it might be possible to form a new club.

During a discussion on a name of the new club, Grose suggested that the club should tactically emulate the style of play used by the Argyll and Sutherland Highlanders, whose team-work in winning the Army Cup had impressed him. At the time they lived in Argyle street in Plymouth and so they decided on the name Plymouth Argyle. From the back of the room a soldier hails 'That is a load of shite, how can we be related to some English team?' I calmly look over and respond saying 'That just shows how ignorant you are about you own Regimental history you fucking retard' which generates a roar of laughter.

The base would soon be enjoying the peace that darkness brings. When darkness comes so must discipline. The base is always in complete blackout during night hours for obvious reasons.

This reminds me of my own stupidity of smoking during our early evacuation.

Plans are already afoot in the ops room for operations tomorrow. Monty and I discuss what he needs medically. He takes Abbie with him and the OMLT have Sean until their patrol medic turns up. Jenny and I cover the medical post here. I realised in the early days that you can't just put everyone out on the ground all of the time. The base has the safest area for helicopters to land and my medics needed someone to send their wounded back to. Major Clark also needed sound advice and answers very quickly about casualties.

Our system ensured that casualties were never left waiting. The base had a basic set up but it afforded the guys a safe haven. They knew that we would be waiting for them and were reassured that we would deploy at a moment's notice to get them if they couldn't make it back.

I make my way to my bed space and look forward to a sound nights sleep. Looking at the state of my socks and get annoyed that our re-supply of personal kit still hasn't arrived. I am surviving on two pairs of pants and socks. I'd always kept them in the bottom of my grab bag and was very thankful that I did. Little things like this made life more bearable. Another day done and dusted.

I put my earphones in and fall asleep to the sounds of my top rated tunes thinking about getting home in one piece. Where else in the world would I want to be? It's not even first light when the blokes start preparing to roll out. We all share some idle chat before they set off. I give Abbie and Sean the normal stay safe routine. One thing that I ensure I always do is leave nothing left unsaid. Out here life can change very quickly and you'd wish that you had always said more. Even a 'Stay safe' is better than nothing at all. Abbie, Sean and Jen were all younger than me and I felt responsible for all of them. If anything happened to them then I would have to face their loved ones and explain myself.

I would be naive to think that it could never be one of them getting hurt. I watch them patrol off into the distance and soak up the quiet that they have left behind. I decide to take a walk around the gun positions to check in with the blokes. It's a welcome break for the Jocks on the wall to have someone else to talk to. We have taken to collecting in breakfast rations in the ops room and cooking them in one of the many used ammunition tins. It's Kev's turn. I hand him my boil in the bag breakfast of sausage and beans before I start my walk round. I put on my body armour and helmet and make my way to the outer wall. This was the safest way to walk round.

It afforded some cover from any stray rounds flying around the base. I chat to the Jocks that are awake and preparing to go on guard. They ask all the usual questions. How long are we here for? When is the next re-supply? Who's the new officer with the OMLT? Referring to Flashheart.

Ham has already given the blokes the lowdown. The young Jocks don't hold back about anything or anyone. Their humour is the one thing that never leaves them, even at their lowest point. I am positive that the end of the world could be inbound and these Jocks would still be taking the piss out of something or someone. By the time I get to the last position it's light and the net is peaceful for a change.

I notice something strange in the last position though. The soldier guarding it is asleep 'What the fuck' I say, putting words to my thoughts. What if I was some crazed Taliban fighter who had found him sleeping? This wasn't some training exercise we were on and this idiot was our last line of defence in the base. I recognize him, it's the fucking armourer and he quickly wakes up as I wade into him with some verbal encouragement in the form of 'What the fuck are you on. Pricks like you are why the infantry trust no one but their own!' I say loudly. He replies with 'Uh, uh, uh, uh' I can see that he is confused which re-affirms the fact that he was asleep.

'You have compromised everyone in this patrol base'. Davey is in charge of the security of the base and wastes no time in involving himself heavily in the situation. We are in Taliban held Nad-e Ali and the thought of the base getting breached didn't even bear thinking about. It would be carnage. Short of shooting one of your own, this is as bad as it gets on operations. You never fall asleep. There is no sympathy and no polite chat. Davey goes ballistic! His boys have been getting thrashed and this clown has only been on stag for half an hour. There are no training instructors out here to put right our mistakes, there are just enemy soldiers waiting to take advantage of them. The armourer was silent and rightly so. As with everything out here a quick resolution is found. The armourer gets to guard his position for six hours instead of two.

This brings joy to the Jocks in his corner as they snigger out of sight of Davey. Jocks will be Jocks after all and laughing at someone else getting thrashed is a feeling I recall myself when I was a junior soldier. In fact I remember doing it not so long ago in the Sgt's Mess so some things will never change. The armourer is never found asleep again strangely enough. Me and Jen turn our attentions to washing ourselves, the best we can. I go through the normal daily rigger of thigh burn in the back of one of the wagons. It feels good though.

Teeth are clean and I am good to go. Scoff is cooking away and I am looking forward to my sausage and beans. We potter about looking for any menial tasks that need doing. The morning goes by without incident. Monty's platoon have been clearing compounds and there are two other call signs in our area. The OMLT are conducting low level ops with the Kandak and there is a police mentor unit en-route from Lash. They have their own compound nearby with the police. Without warning three loud explosions are followed by the sound of heavy machine gun bursts can be heard close by. The radio net goes crazy and the base is silenced. Captain Wood checks in with Monty and he reports no activity from the enemy.

He then checks in with Flashheart and again he reports no enemy activity. The 'Throatcutters' call sign has been heavily ambushed on the way in to our location. One of their vehicles has taken a direct hit from an RPG. They are under heavy fire and have taken multiple casualties. It's just me and Jen in the medical room so we know that we are going to be up against it. We prepare ourselves and initiate Nine Liners early to warn Bastion that we have casualties in bound. It's a waiting game as these lads need to get back to the patrol base so we can stabilise them and then evacuate them by air.

We wait at least 15 minutes before they appear at the gate. There are four guys badly wounded one of them more than the others. An Afghan Special Forces soldier has been KIA (Killed in Action). We get the injured in and get to work. A couple are hurt pretty bad, the Afghan soldiers bring the dead soldier in and place him in the middle of the room. I notice that they think he is still alive. He has been shot through the head so there is blood is everywhere. The Afghans gather around their dead soldier and start fussing around him. They check his airway and try to move him. I have the unfortunate task of pronouncing the soldier dead. It's not the norm but we have no doctor to do it. His head injury is very severe and there is no output whatsoever. His pupils are fixed. I feel for the Afghans who surround his body.

It's their comrade and friend lying there and they don't want to believe that he can't be helped. The Afghans deal with their dead in their own way so I suggest that they take his body to prepare him for the MERT flight. I try to be as gentle as possible with them as I know they feel the loss the same as we would. I spot one of the police mentoring team from Lash, so it was a relief to see that he was okay. He was very calm and helped us tend to the wounded and prepare them for evacuation. These guys had already received basic first aid on the ground.

We checked the tourniquets and made sure that fractured limbs were splinted. The boss peers around the corner of the doorway, he looks at the carnage before him and I can see he is taken aback. He gives me a sort of nod of appreciation. He knew that this wasn't a great situation and probably felt a bit sorry for us.

I know that he needs information fast to relay over the net back to Brigade HQ. He is being as diplomatic as the situation will allow. But he is under pressure from Brigade and Bastion to get information. This in turn will allow them to make their decisions and warn off relevant surgeons to prepare for the wounded. I have no plans on keeping these boys for long. An orthopaedic surgeon will be far more useful than me or Jen. I make the call that they are stable enough to fly to Bastion. The boss gives the nod and disappears next door to the ops room.

For the four casualties that we have there are another three or so with less obvious wounds. Blasts often cause tertiary injuries in people close to the explosion so these guys needed to be evacuated also. I can't risk recalling the MERT for slow developing chest injuries as intelligence is giving some worrying information about the Taliban's future intentions and targets. So the number of casualties goes up to seven plus one KIA.

The MERT are on route so we finish up and prepare to move them to the landing zone (LZ). It takes a lot of us to carry the five stretchers. Bearing in mind numbers in the base are declining and fast. Blokes are woken from their rest periods to help. They get up without question they know that every man there would do the same if it was them lying on the stretcher. Soldiers will moan with the best of them until someone gets injured.

This isn't a good start to the day and a little unexpected if I'm honest. We make it across to the LZ and wait patiently for wheels down. I start thinking about stretchers and the fact that we are running short. I ask Davey to grab a stretcher off the Chinook and I will do the same. Wheels are down and we start hauling the casualties on including our dead. The handover is done and I reach out to grab a stretcher. A member of the MERT gestures for me not to take one. This catches me unaware. Did I just see that or am I hallucinating? No! It's real. I'm in no mood to be told by some RAF nurse that I am only allowed to take one stretcher. Especially when she can replenish her stock of stretchers upon her return to Bastion. I wonder if they maybe have to go somewhere else first. We've got men on the ground and I am running dangerously low on stretchers. If ever there was a time that I wanted to inflict violence on a complete stranger then this was that time!

What the fuck? I raged inside and snatched the stretcher out of her hand and aggressively pointed to the stretchers that we had just loaded on. Including our dead! The noise on a Chinook is loud so words cannot be heard. Emotions were running high and in my heightened state I felt angry that she thought that this was appropriate behaviour at such a desperate time.

I sprint off the ramp and take cover while it lifts off. Weren't we supposed to be on the same side? This was turning into a shite day and fast. First the armourer asleep on stag and now the stretcher police. I head back to the base muttering a host of profanities to myself. One of the Brit mentoring team starts to tell me how he was on top cover just seconds before the Afghan soldier was shot in the head. They had just changed over!

The guys were cleaning out the wagon which was covered in blood. The dead soldier's helmet was retrieved and unfortunately still had part of his head left in it. Davey decided to bury it as a mark of respect. All British soldiers are made aware of local Afghan cultures prior to arriving in Helmand and know that if a body or body parts are found and there is time it should be buried in a respectful manner.

I think that regardless of how mentally tough you think you are when it's your guys that are bleeding you feel pretty vulnerable and I did that day.

My desire for not wanting to hear someone else's war stories had gone. I wanted to hear anyone else's story but my own. I wasn't interested in B Company holding Nad-e Ali.

The mission to get the turbine to Kajaki Dam couldn't be further from my thoughts. I felt dejected and uncharacteristically negative. I was angry that we were always on the receiving end. Every day we were getting hit and every other day we were taking casualties; we didn't have the kit or capabilities to sustain any of it. The Osprey body armour that we had been issued was not holding up to the job at hand.

I had invested in Blackhawk pouches that fitted the armour much better and I was thankful to have done so. It dawned on me that all this agitation was covering my concern about losing one of our own. I didn't want to acknowledge the black body bags underneath the old desk in the corner of the aid post. B Company had grown close and I had started to look at a lot of the guys as family.

I went back to the medical room, it was like a scene from a horror film, with blood everywhere after the treatment of the injured. Jen and I scrub it with what we have. We do this in silence of course, all very British and stiff upper lip. Sometimes saying nothing is better, a big fat discussion was the last thing we needed.

Worse was still to come for the Police Mentoring Team (PMT) who had to make their way back to Lash after being smashed on the way in. Strangely enough they were smashed on the way back out as well. They reported back minor casualties but cracked on.

It seemed that the Taliban were cutting off our supply lines which was bad news. They had littered most of the routes with IEDs, so road moves became impossible. Disruption can sometimes be a far more effective weapon than rockets. All of the wars in history could tell you that.

Surprisingly Monty's crew had been left alone as were Flashheart's Kandak. The Taliban had already had their success today. Later that evening we endured a small arms attack but compared to earlier events it was pretty tame. The Taliban body count was already at 30, somehow though the fighters still came.

Earlier in the tour the Americans flooded Garmsir, a town which lies on the southern tip of Helmand Province. They deployed more than 2,000 US Marines in the form of 24 Marine Expeditionary Unit; together with A Company of 5 Scots they drove the Taliban out of Garmisir. This had ultimately forced the insurgents to find another route up to the Sangin Valley. Marjah and Nad-e Ali have become the Taliban's new highway to hell.

We welcome Monty's platoon back in to the base. They can't believe that they missed all the drama. There is a lot to talk about and our room stays lively until around 2000 hrs. Every roll mat in the base is full apart from the radio stag and the Jocks on the wall. We work a rotation to cover the radio net, doing two hours at night and two hours in the day, I am on death stag tonight and it's hard to stay focused. This is when you smoke cigarettes just to keep yourself conscious. Radio checks take place every fifteen minutes. I wondered if anyone in Brigade Headquarters had actually woken up to the fact that we were in a world of shite down here. It seemed that the turbine move up north was taking all of the news. The latest rumour was that 3 Para were being sent down here to boost numbers and conduct offensive operations.

The Pathfinder Platoon (PF) were also rumoured to be conducting offensive ops in Marjah, this would hopefully smash the Taliban before they got to Nad-e Ali. I start to run through some ridiculous trains of thought whilst listening to the white noise of the radio. What if we got stuck out here or the Marines somehow couldn't get in? What if the base gets overrun or one of our helicopters gets shot down? This is what happens when you get the radio watch in the early hours, the death stag. This is the sort of crap that was now filling my pickled brain.

It's dark and quiet so I keep a constant paranoid watch on the entrance to the makeshift ops room. Any shadows are starting to look like potential threats. My rifle is in my lap. I remind myself of an incident that took place up north in one of the Forward Operating Bases. One of the Afghan soldiers decided to fire a burst into a room where some of 2 Para were sleeping. He shot three of them, thankfully none of them were killed. Good time to think about it though. My stag is coming to an end and it's definitely time for some bivvy bag action to clear the nonsense out of my now pan-fried head. Jen's on stag next so I wake her as quietly as I can. That's probably the worst sound that any soldier will ever hear. Someone whispering 'Your stag'. I hated it when I joined up and I hate it now! The white noise from the radio continues as I lay my head, it takes at least another hour before I can doze off.

CHAPTER FIVE

Face to Face with the Taliban

Overnight as if by magic a shower unit has appeared in the middle of the base, it reminds me of a tipi, the type of shelter you find at the Glastonbury festival, all it is missing is a sign saying 'shower'. Since our arrival no one has been able to have a proper wash, most of us had taken to using the multi-purpose yellow sharps container and a flannel or small cloth. You get used to being grubby and once you get to the stage when you are comfortable that you stink, you are no longer as bothered as you really should be.

Kev and I sit quietly relaxing in the Ops room. The boss is enjoying his first shower and Captain Wood is reading outside. Day dreaming on my roll mat, I wonder what may become of us down here. My moment of peace is interrupted by a conversation which I hear developing outside. Flashheart is discussing how the lack of amenities must be taking its toll on the men of B Company, worse still for the females attached. Kev looks at me with a smirk, clearly knowing that I will have something to say about it.

I ignore the conversation until the role of woman on the frontline is raised. Kev's smirk is now a full on Chelsea smile. I smile back knowing that I am far too relaxed to engage in shite chat with Flashheart so early in the morning. I hold out for a whole two minutes until Flashheart appears in my peripheral vision, it was only a matter of time before he would start to annoy me, I think.

'So Sgt Taylor, what do you think?'

'What about, Sir?' I reply.

'Uh, uh about woman serving in the Infantry?'

I pause for a second looking at the floppy haired officer before me, I scan his kit and scrutinise the way he is dressed. I get eyes on two knee pads, one on each knee. No one ever wears two knee pads, well unless you are busy doing stuff you shouldn't be. I only packed one knee pad as had the rest of B Company. If he was diffusing a bomb then maybe he would be forgiven. I am surprised he is not wearing a full set of Gortex just in case it rains.

This told me all I needed to know about Flashheart so I was now ready to engage in his shit chat. Without too much thought my reply is clear and unwavering.'From my experience I am not keen, however if it is about choice and maybe certain roles could open up. Although, there are plenty of weak men to be carried already aren't there Sir?'

Blushing slightly there was no comeback to my statement only laughter from the second in command outside. Captain Wood and I had forged a good working relationship; we had already had this conversation. He knew me and my team well and had come to rely on us as we did him. We spent much time in Nawa (a district to the north of Garmsir) together. He was a witty young officer who I was sure was destined for great things.

When I hear liberals having their often heavy debates about equality in the Armed Forces, I often think; send your daughter or sister to the frontline or better still send yourself and soak up a bit of the atmospherics of Nad-e Ali, Sangin or Marjah then you can make an informed decision. There are a few females who have the stomach to push a bayonet into another person, twist it, take it out and do it again, to make sure that the enemy is dead.

Those types are few and far between. Female soldiers already play a key role in many areas of the military. From intelligence work, technical areas, dog handling, command positions, as fighter pilots, and of course medicine. In Helmand some of the bravest young soldiers are females driving supply lorries across open desert constantly facing Taliban attack. Then of course there are the frontline medics who serve with the MERT or on the ground.

(*above.*)
The WMIK Land Rover which was first deployed in 2006 and has been constantly used with great effect. By 2011 the standard of protected vehicles had been significantly increased.

(*above.*)
Snatch Land Rovers, the box body on the back offered little protection against attack and those inside often cooked in the Helmand heat. The Snatch was upgraded by the MoD in a new variant called Vixen.

(*above.*)
On patrol across the scorching Helmand desert. A view from the top of a
WMIK Land Rover.

(*left*.)
Me, left with LCpl
Farrell Foy, helps a
wounded Afghan
to the medical
room at Lashkar
Gah. The base at
Lash was also the
headquarters of the
Brigade.

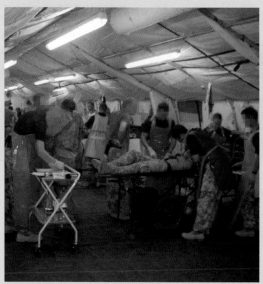

(*left*.)
Inside the
British military
field hospital in
Bastion in 2006,
where I worked.

(*above.*)
Cpl Stuart Pearson, now Sgt, receives his QGM from the
Queen. Stu had 14 different injuries from the mine strike near
the Kajaki Dam.

(*right.*)
Cpl Mark Wright,
lost his life in the
minefield at Kajaki.
He was awarded
the George Cross
for his outstanding
courage and
bravery.

(*above.*)
OMLT Medic LCpl Gurung was wounded in blue on blue/green incident involving the UGLY call sign (the Apache).

(*right.*)
Me, before it all gets a bit serious on the canal track leading to NAWA district, this notorious stretch of road was littered with IEDs.

(*above.*)
Finding the time and space to shelter from the midday heat with Sgt Scotty Mcfadden.

(*below.*)
Boydy enjoying a pre-evacuation cigarette.

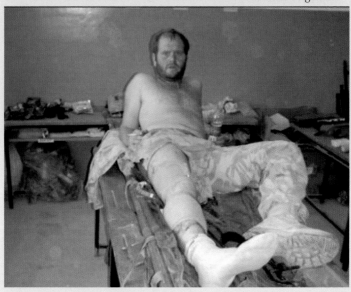

(*above.*)
Cpl James Henderson manning one of the Heavy Machine Guns, which was sited in a corner of our makeshift Patrol Base. This was the place where I used to make calls home.

(*left.*)
The photo of my brother Dave that I kept on the inside of my body armour along with my lucky rosary beads.

(*above.*)
OC 'B Company' Major Harry
Clark, Kev and me re-group after
the Taliban attack in the Afghan
district centre of Nade-ali.

(*below.*)
B Company Medics from left to
right: LCpl Sean Maloney, Pte Abbie
Cottle, me and LCpl Jenny Young.

(*left.*)
B Company
Sgt Major
WO2 (CSM)
Davey
Robertson
resting after
another long
event-filled
day.

(*below.*)
'Days like this'. Hendy, Coaksee and Baz after the 1.5
km casualty extraction under fire when they carried
Boydy.

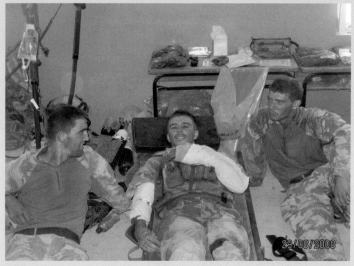

(*above.*)
Cpl Tam Rankine flanked by Cpl Scotty Pew and Cpl James Henderson.
Their leadership under fire was never less than outstanding.

(*left.*)
The
charismatic
platoon Sgt
'Monty'
Monteith -
patrolling in
Nad-e Ali.

(*left*.)
The minimal medical kit in our Company Aid Post.

(*below*.)
The four medics, me, Jen, Abbie and Sean in Nade-ali.

(*above.*)
The RAF C-130 Hercules, which initially used to ferry home wounded
soldiers either from Camp Bastion or Kandahar. It was later replaced by
the C-17.

(*below.*)
Troops pour into the back of a Chinook, the workhorse of Helmand.
Since 2006 the RAF airframe has supported infantry missions and
medical evacuation with many pilots being decorated for their bravery

(right.)
Original casualty list.

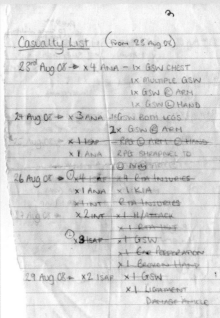

Casualty List (From 23 Aug 08)

23rd Aug 08 → x4 ANA — 1x GSW CHEST
                        1x MULTIPLE GSW
                        1x GSW ® ARM
                        1x GSW Ⓛ HAND

24 Aug 08 → x3 ANA — GSW BOTH LEGS
                     2x GSW ® ARM
          → x1 ISAF — RPG ® ARM ⊕ HAND
            x1 ANA — RPG SHRAPNEL TO
                     ⊕ ARM

26 Aug 08 → ① x4 — ①4 RTA INJURIES
            x1 ANA — x1 KIA
            x1 INT — RTA INJURIES

27 Aug 08 → x2 INT — x1 H/ATTACK
                     x1 RTA INJ
          ① x3 ISAF — x1 GSW
                     x1 EYE PERFORATION
                     x1 BROKEN HAND

29 Aug 08 → x2 ISAF — x1 GSW
                     x1 LIGAMENT
                     DAMAGE ANKLE

(below.)
Fighting Platoon chain of command. 2Lt Simon Du Boulay and Monty.

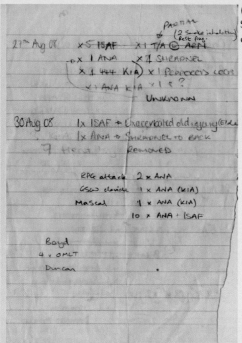

(*left.*)
Second half of the
casualty list.

(*above.*) Ali Cat enjoying my chicken and herb Army ration cat food.

(*above.*) 18 year old Duffy chose Helmand as his first operational tour.

(*below.*) Lt Barclay with the offending belt of 7.62 mm ammunition.

(*right.*)
My good friend Sgt Phil Train of 2 PARA.

(*below.*)
The blokes during some down time, Geordie making short work of an Andy McNab book.

In Helmand, we have been forced to squeeze into the frontline because we have so few troops trying to stabilise the area. For many years we had more than 20,000 in Northern Ireland, yet when we first deployed to southern Afghanistan we sent just 4,500 troops and it took several years before that was uplifted to 10,000.

As a force we simply cannot provide the 'safe and secure environment' to allow reconstruction to take place. All the humanitarian efforts are futile if the insurgency is allowed to continue and in some cases expand.

The only way, in my opinion that the UK could have delivered success in Southern Afghanistan would have been to surge troops to at least 30,000. Then in the early years we may have been able to hold on to the ground that had been fought and died for. Our soldiers should never have been exposed to situations where they are outnumbered by the enemy.

In 2006, 40 Paratroopers were isolated for more than a month in the district centre in Musa Qaleh. The men against all odds held the base only to see it handed back to Taliban control six months later. How can that be explained? Who makes the decision. There was no strategic gain for handing it back; the ever so important 'bigger picture' wasn't gaining either. We the Brits were trying to secure a country twice the size of Wales.

The UK Government did not increase troop numbers to any significant level until 2008, perhaps through fear of losing public support. This may have been generated by concern that Britain would see more soldiers killed. In the end the US had to come into Helmand.

The lefties in Government have all but destroyed the fabric of Great Britain. We needed Churchill back, a Brit who knew how to take care of business overseas. Relaxing again I make a cup of tea, I am joined by Abbie and Jen, we discuss the wish list of kit that should be arriving in the re-supply. Just when I thought it was safe to relax Flashheart saunters into the ops room holding what looks like a small French coffee press. 'Anyone for coffee?'

I look at Abbie who in turn looks at Jen. We all look at Kev and the sniggering starts. Shaking my head I politely decline his offer and bury my head in my bivvy bag. Flashheart sips his coffee, smoking his Marlboro Light cigarette on the bench outside.

He looks just as comfortable here in Nad-e Ali as I'm sure he would be sat outside a pub in the West End of London. His annoying aura actually makes him quite interesting to me, I find myself continuing to watch him as he cuts about the place. It passes time and gives me something else to think about. Anything that takes your mind off Nad-e Ali for a while is welcome.

The moment is interrupted the radio net becomes busy we hear a contact report from that a friendly call sign. A British unit has reported heavy fighting in Marjah to our south. Our quiet time is on hold as we listen to the drama unfolding. 'We were lucky down there mucker' Kev says 'I know mate, let's hope they are too eh?' I reply.

B Company had not long returned from the Nawa district, south of Helmand's capital Lashkar Gah, when we were sent down to an unknown area of operations in Marjah. I had deployed as the lead B Company medic along with the command group. I was top cover with Kev who was the OC's TAC signaller. I am not sure if it's right for medics or attached arms to be on top cover, but at the end of the day no one is adding value sat in the back of a vehicle when there are arcs to be covered through the top of the turrets. The road move to Marjah was a long slow process. Every few hundred yards we have to stop at what are considered to be Vulnerable Points (VP) where the Taliban might attack us or plant IEDs. We get out and search the ground with mine detectors and check for booby traps. It is a life saving process , which we call Op Barma. This drill was enforced at almost every vulnerable point. No one on the patrol enjoys the time consuming task, but everyone understands how important it is.

Having just lost three lads and the first female soldier no one complained that we were being cautious. Members of our own company had been hit prior to our trip to Marjah, that's how I came to be on these patrols in the first place, we needed medical cover. Cpl Neil Mckenzie who was B Company's lead medic, had been injured when he was thrown out of the WMIK that was hit. He and a couple of others were extremely lucky to survive that day.

The heat from the sun made the journey at times unbearable, with nowhere to shelter you are sometimes at the mercy of cloudless blue skies. A trick I had learnt in the jungle of Sierra Leone helped to keep our water supply at a decent temperature. The key was to drench an old sock in water and then place the warm bottle inside of it. The heat in the water evaporates into the sock leaving the water relatively cool. It was a small luxury that made life in the desert heat bearable. I also took my multi-purpose yellow sharps container. If we are out for a few days then I need something to use as a makeshift toilet. This and the back of our wagon worked perfectly. Initially we stayed in the open desert outside of Marjah. Our mission was to probe and report on atmospherics and any activity in the area. During intelligence briefs Marjah had been identified as a haven for insurgents intent on the cultivation of poppies.

Our operation was set over several days. At night we would use the desert as a makeshift base. It provides clear 360 arcs so an all-round defence stance was adopted. On the first day of the patrol I saw a suspect vehicle full of what we considered fighting aged males. It went tearing past our convoy between 500 and 600 metres away. It got everyone's attention and was a small combat indicator for what was yet to come. During dark hours the general routine would normally be to rest around our vehicles, eating our shite scoff, covering radio stag after last light and waiting for sunrise.

During the hottest part of the day we would try to find shade and in the middle of the desert that task can be interesting. I remember finding that the coolest place was down beside one of the Land Rover wheels; I somehow managed to squeeze my 5 feet 8 inches frame into that tiny shadow. After several days half the company were given orders to return to Lash, the rest of us would continue to probe in and around the outskirts of Marjah.

That night we took some Indirect Fire or IDF on our desert leger, it wasn't particularly close but it felt to me like a warning and it was close enough to force us to move one or two kilometres away. We continued to probe and focused our attention closer now in search of any signs of obvious enemy activity.

The heat was at times crippling. My Sierra Leone trick stopped as I could not justify the use of water to dampen the sock. Drinking warm water in extreme heat is enough to make you vomit.

It's hard to explain but the heat more than anything makes these patrols tough. The vehicles were like ovens, it was soul destroying and that's before anything even happens. Throughout our time in Marjah I always felt that something was going to happen and the longer we stayed the stronger that feeling got. Orders came from command that we were to probe into the centre of Marjah and everyone on the patrol knew that the situation was not at all positive. The mixture of excitement and fear is something very hard to put into words.

My palms were sweaty, I was thirsty and yet for some reason I couldn't wait to get into Marjah. We moved off slowly and purposefully. It wasn't long before the first IED was discovered. The mine clearing equipment we use is based on the same principals as the machines used by enthusiasts that search for old coins and metals. During a routine Op Barma drill I recall thinking this isn't right. I could sense that something was wrong. The smell of cooking reminded me of the time of day. It was getting close to lunch and with that the heat was ever increasing.

As we turned onto one of the tracks which lead onto the canal, I could see local villagers running and they weren't running towards us they were running away. I looked at Kev saying 'We are gonna get fucking smashed here'. Kev laughed nervously, he knew I was right and we were just wondering where it would come from. I was constantly scanning all around and wondering what was going to happen.

If I am honest I would say that my excitement had very positively disappeared and the fear kicked right in. My legs felt like jelly I now wanted something to happen just so I could feel or think about something else. We were at that point again where the anticipation is worse than the event. Kev is my battle buddy on this mission, he is fiercely proud of being an Argyll. I trust him implicitly and hoped that it wasn't us getting hit first. 'IED or small arms?' I whisper quietly to Kev. I didn't have to wait long for my answer. Our convoy crawled onto the Canal track and started to push slowly down the side of it. We had no choice, our patrol was committed. Kev and I were in the second vehicle. The local villagers continued to run and then the place erupted. Boom! Boom! Two deafening explosions were followed rapidly by small arms fire and heavy machine guns. The familiar airburst of incoming rocket propelled grenades rained debris and shrapnel all around us.

The convoy came to a grinding halt. Kev and I were shunted forward into the metal ledge in front of us. We were taking sustained and heavy fire from every direction. Smoke began to fill the air, making it somehow hotter than before. Rounds started pinging off the top of our vehicle and I remember seeing them zip through the antenna above me. Within seconds the mounted guns on our WMIKs roared into action. The sound was unbelievable.

Kev and I had immediately taken cover, ducking down inside the hatch. Looking up I could see that the rounds were coming in from left to right, from my side of the wagon. They zipped past so quickly that it made all of my own movements feel like I was in slow motion. I couldn't move fast enough.

Our vehicles could not withstand small arms fire for long so we had to react. I popped back up and immediately got eyes on a Taliban fighter, he was just over 30 metres away half right of me in a field to our left. It happened very quickly, I engaged him, firing seven shots which would later become quite the joke within my Regiment. Apparently I was wasting ammunition. The first two were hazy, I just fired in his general direction then I could see him clearly. I could see his baggy clothing which was darker than the colour of the field that he was standing in.

His face was long, this exaggerated by a straggly black beard. The one thing that struck me was the fearlessness in him. He wasn't looking directly at me but he knew the odds were he was about to die. He continued to fire elaborate drug crazed bursts from his AK47.

I shouted half a fire control order but it wasn't anything like the ones that I had taught recruits to use. It was desperate and I almost had the urge to point. Kev and the Minimi gunner in the vehicle behind ours got eyes on more fighters in the same field.

The fighter that I had engaged had dropped, and by that time I too was looking to engage others. It would never be right to claim a kill as a medic but at the end of the day he no longer had the ability to engage us and that's all that I was concerned about. Faced with the choice of him or me , I chose me.

The Taliban had timed their attack on us perfectly. They chose the hottest part of the day which was just another tactic to slow us, 'the infidels' down. It would give them time to at least maim or kill a few of us.

'Man Down! Man Down!' I could hear the radio traffic through the back of the vehicle. The boss and driver are still in the front. Major Clark shouts through to the back. 'One casualty in the rear vehicle Sgt T' He jumps out as I climb through the back door of the vehicle to meet him.

From there we start to run towards the rear of the convoy. I become very aware that we are visibly open to the enemy fire, and even more open to the rays of the midday heat. My medical pack suddenly feels like it is housing a fridge freezer. Midway along the track the boss stops and turns back towards our vehicle. I don't ask why I just follow him, it's not through lack of interest, my lungs needed oxygen far more than they needed a conversation. I jump back into the wagon and struggle to breathe. 'You okay mucker?' Kev laughs. I want to share the joke with him and the fact that I was in and out of our vehicle like a fucking yoyo, but I was still struggling for air, our vehicle shunts forward as we hastily move off.

Back on top cover I can't cool down, I want to take my helmet off but don't. Slowly I re-compose myself. Kev is still laughing at my ordeal of running in the midday heat. All soldiers are the same worldwide. I laughed at friends of mine getting beasted up and downs hills with a GPMG in Brecon. It's always funny when it's not you on the receiving end. We stop near some open ground and two B Company snipers set up on the roof of a compound nearby. Pte Russell King, 'Kingy' is a young Jock from Stirling. Our Company snipers are a godsend along with the 'Ugly' call sign now on station, the Apache.

The Apache which has arrived above us sets about hunting the Taliban of Marjah. The insurgents here weren't rag tag, they knew what they were doing, and they had just educated us in a textbook L - Shaped ambush, from the left and the rear. The soldier that has been hit is Chucky, a tiny Scot, who has been shot in the abdomen; LCpl Tom Rooke (Rookey) has been taking care of him. Chucky had been manning the .50 calibre machine gun and the entry wound looks pretty high so I am inclined to think that he may be developing chest wound. The Nine Liner goes out and he is sent as urgent surgical, Chucky needs a hasty evacuation.

Our company snipers along with the Apache get busy to shield the casevac now under fire. Kev is busy on the net and the rest of the company provide an all-round defence. The Chinook comes in swift and heavy. I attach Chuckie's paperwork to his chest and grab the first person that comes off the bird. I scream all the important stuff in his ear and hope that he gets the bit about my concern for Chuckie's chest. He gives me the thumbs up and heads back up the ramp followed by his force protection. As the Chinook takes off again, I look around at the faces of our company. It's not such a great feeling being left in Marjah knowing that we had to somehow get ourselves out of this shit hole and back to Lashkar Gah.

We had the Apache to escort us out of Marjah, small arms fire ever present. We make the desert leger unscathed and head back to the PB. Me and Kev are all but silent on the way back, minimal chat or banter this time we were tired.

You were right mucker' Kev says.

'How?' I reply.

'About us getting smashed' Kev smiles.

I could taste the salt on the skin around my mouth, before heading back I empty a rehydration sachet into my now boiling hot bottle of water. Not a wet sock in sight. A perfect way to end a perfect day I thought.

Sandbag chat over and back to the reality and the peace of Patrol Base Argyll. Resting on my bivvy, I catch a glimpse of Captain Wood. He always finds ways to amuse himself, he is busy in his own little routine and I notice that he has the red iPod. FlashHeart's red iPod has become part of the bloke's normal routine, I am humoured that he thinks it's his own little secret. Having grown up in a household with three older brothers I have seen and heard worse I am sure.

I watch everyone going about their business, almost forgetting to do my own chores half a world away I inspect my feet. I don't think the offer of being a foot model is coming my way any time soon. I am amazed at the resilience of the young Jocks.

They are surviving as best they know how, we all are. I am drawn to the ordinarily common events they make fun of. Someone only has to trip over in a gun position or say something remotely feminine for the place to erupt with laughter. The banter is something else. They abuse each other all day long. It is what gets them in, fact all of us, through the day. There's a strange bond between them. One minute you could be the subject of ridicule and the next minute you could have been wounded, getting carried two miles by your section because when you get hurt, the lads get straight back to the serious business of being there for each other.

Captain Wood is all over the fact that a much needed injection of morale is required to motivate individuals carrying out the mundane tasks of equipment husbandry outside in the area housing the WMIKs. 'Sgt T' he says with a smile 'I think you may be developing a man-crush on Flashheart'. Ham jumps on the bandwagon adding 'Aye sir that's why she keeps going on about him, she's after his other knee pad'

Laughing I shake my head, I was in a no-win situation so I just went with it 'Maybe I do have a man crush on Flashheart, so what?' I try to remain stern faced but one look at Ham has me giggling. 'You are a dick Ham, but you are right about the knee pad. Flashheart is the alliest man on camp' I say laughing.

For a moment morale was lifted, soldiers never let the truth get in the way of a good joke. Everyone eagerly waits for another re-supply. Information relayed over the net says that the mentoring team's medic is inbound. Happy Days, that means that I get Sean back. The Afghan Special Forces are sending a team out with two British mentors from the OMLT. Low on manpower Davey needs a hand to co-ordinate getting these guys off the helicopter and back to the base. I get my kit on preparing myself for the trip out. Monty is taking a well-earned break and is sleeping in the aid post.

He and his men have been getting smashed these last few days. I am becoming more aware of just how much the boss achieves with this company, albeit not at full strength. Once every mission is complete the boss ensures that there is a value adding debrief, no bullshit just anything that went well and anything that could be done better.

When his men stand down that's exactly what they get, he leaves them alone. They respond by giving him total respect and 100% effort every time. The loyalty in this company is unbelievable. Just like the days of the Great War, these Jocks depend on each other and will die for one another without question. That's a rare commodity in this day and age, I often chat with Monty about home and what he will do when he gets there.

His is an old fashioned family man who misses his wife and two daughters. He keeps a picture of his wife and girls beside his roll mat, as does Davey. We have become a tight-knit group, the lads of B Company are genuine and I think a lot of them for it. Heading out to the landing site I catch up with Davey at the gate. He has been given wheels up from Bastion so the Helo will be inbound shortly.

As we take up our positions I see that Davey is very close to where the bird normally sits when it lands. It's dark so his shadow is illuminated by the cylums. With the threat of attack on our helicopter so high a short period of time on the ground is paramount. The co-ordination must be exact and seem less. The Chinook lands heavy onto the ground, large crates are dropped first followed by my medic and the guys mentoring the Afghan team. I grab hold of the first man and instruct him to follow me and stay close.

Getting off a helicopter into an unknown area can be disorientating, that's why I must guide them in. The Chinook lifts off as we make our way back into the patrol base, Davey jokes that he was nearly squashed by the Chinook, reaffirming my earlier thought that he was way too close to where the bird normally sits. His team get busy sorting the stores and Ham does his usual quad and trailer stuff .

But he still has time to mock Davey for his near death experience. I get back to the ops rooms with the new guys, as I take off my helmet they look shocked to be met by a woman. I introduce myself in what now feels like an awkward first date and hand them over to Major Clark. I take one of the mentors to where they will be housed along with their Afghan team. He asks me how long we had been here for. I give him the lowdown of our time in Nad-e Ali thus far. Making my way back to the ops room I see that Davey is unpacking the stores so I join the team and help out. It's been nearly three weeks and finally our kit has arrived.

Colleagues back in Lash had packed our bergens (back packs) and sent them down to us. I am excited that I will now have at least three pairs of socks and an equal amount of pants. Mega! I pull out a clean T-shirt that smells of washing powder. It reminds me of home. I have been planning to use the newly erected shower and looked forward to tomorrow morning. I snuggle down with my softie sleeping bag what a treat. I am asleep within seconds and don't stir until first light, yes that was only four hours away but it felt longer. The patrol base is alive this morning. With an extra spring in their step every man was excited about socks and pants. If I were anywhere else doing something different, these basic things wouldn't even cross my mind.

Out here though the sight of shower gel was like the discovery of the Holy Grail. My planned use of the shower is already on hold. A long queue has formed including the new arrivals. These two probably only showered six hours ago and here they were wanting another one. Myself, Jen and Abbie sit patiently outside the med room waiting our turn. It crosses my mind that the cubicle is in open ground, next to the mortar line. The thought of taking a round while covered in soap suds suddenly decreases my desire to get in it. We busy ourselves making scoff and a quick brew.

Then as I hand Abbie my ration pack I notice one of our visitors has decided against having a shower and is now having a strip wash right in front of us. Like cavewoman we all instinctively look at him. It was a genuinely funny moment we had all gone into bloke mode. The sight before us was far easier on the eye than Ferris's lily white arse that was for sure.

Snapping quickly back into reality I realised that my sausage and beans were far more important. One by one everyone got some much needed shower time, it had definitely been worth the wait. I was reluctant to wash my hair at first as it had styled itself into a manageable birds nest, but it had to be done. Today, planning has started on upcoming operations that the company must mount on Taliban strongholds in Nad-e Ali.

The boss is focused and had been given orders from command about key objectives that he must achieve. The area of Shin Kalay keeps appearing on the operations board, Shin Kalay was a Taliban haven and Brigade Headquarters wanted us to patrol into the area to draw the Taliban out. The trouble with that is that the enemy know these areas far better than we do. It has become apparent that the higher echelons were expecting a little too much from the troops on the ground. This type of patrolling was risky; our numbers were dwindling so the gain did not outweigh the risk.

The calculation seemed disjointed. Monty looks tired this morning, he and Lt Du Boulay have been commanding the fighting troops between them for quite some time. Du Boulay borrows my single knee pad for most of his patrols; I suggest that should the worst happen Flashheart will have his second one at hand to give to anyone who required it. Lt Du Boulay thanks me for the suggestion and moves off with Abbie in tow. She is out this morning so I say my goodbyes and get back into the medical room with Jen and Sean and Gurung our new OMLT medic. Gurung is a part of our Squadron back in Colchester so it's great to have him on board. The patrol gets 50 metres out of Argyll before the rounds start pinging around the base. We are under attack and it's come at a random time today.

The PB has been caught unaware and it's not long before I hear the strained screams of 'Medic! Medic!' Looking out from my cover I see that one of the Afghan soldiers has been hit. His team carry him to the medical room, it was pointless pushing too many people out in the open as we were still taking incoming. The soldier wasn't wearing his body armour or helmet and has taken a round through the upper chest. We drag him in and get to work. There is no exit wound; the round must have travelled through some key organs, causing a fair amount of mess not visible to my anxious eyes.

Our systematic approach to casualties is what makes these situations work. A casualty in freefall requires quick if any interventions if life is to be sustained. Maybe a sub-clavian artery is clipped? we treat as we find. I want make sure we do everything we can so I go through the detail of the MARCH - P process.

M – Initial diagnosis amounts to an Internal bleed not visible to the eye. One entry no exit wound. Sitting the casualty up alleviates any chest bleed. Chest seal in place covering entry hole.

A – Quick insertion of a nasopharangeal tube, Jen maintains the casualties airway. I continue to run through possibilities.

R – Listening for breath sounds in a combat environment is not without its problems. Casualty is not breathing and the side of injury is dull on percussion. Jen assists ventilations and Gurung carries out needle decompression to injured side to buy us some time whilst we set about preparing an improvised chest drain. Further diagnosis indicates possible Pneumo/ Haemophorax, this is a mixture of air and blood possibly trapped in the pleural space and chest cavity with no chance to escape. This will result in compression of the heart and lungs ultimately causing death.

C – Major bleed, casualty is in Hypovalemic shock, which in laymans terms means blood loss amounting to low blood volume, a team medic gains IV access, patient has shut down and goes into Cardiac arrest.

CPR or Cardio Pulmonary Resuscitation starts and blood begins to push out of the small hole in the chest wall. Eyes are fixed, pupils are unresponsive, no pulse. No defibrillator at point of wounding, manual CPR is continued.

Although hopeless, it would be insensitive to stop so we crack on for the sake of the troops around us. Lt Col Nazim the Kandak commander is with us throughout the ordeal, the other Afghan soldiers are helping to pass kit and equipment to my medics.

The medical room is full of armed and highly emotional Afghans I take this into consideration as I decide to call time on our efforts to resuscitate the soldier. We do not have the luxury of an endless array of kit, I instruct Jenny to stop with the use of our single chest drain. It would achieve nothing; we could not turn off the tap inside the body so the soldier had basically bled out internally.

With a lump in my throat I tell my medics to stop. I check for any signs of output finally checking his pupils. It's a bad moment for us all; I express my sympathy to the Kandak commander and his men. I update the boss who in turn updates Brigade Headquarters. They will call off the Chinook and MERT team and wait for a suitable time to retrieve the soldier. His comrades take his now lifeless body away to wrap him and pray. The bright start to the day had most definitely darkened. My medics looked deflated. It didn't matter what uniform he was wearing, his loss was shared by us all. It could have been any of us lying there.

We start the task of cleaning up and to be honest I was getting sick of the sight and smell of blood. It was becoming too much of the norm, we sort through the medical kit quickly and at the back of my mind I know that the day is far from over. It has been full on and I am very tired.

We have a patrol out on the ground so I move to the ops room to listen to their progress on the net. It appears that our call sign is already in trouble. The intelligence passed down to us indicates that the Taliban already has eyes on Du Boulay and his men. They continue to push forward patrolling into an inevitable ambush. As crazy as it sounds these are directives from command. They have air support which will allow enemy positions identified to be taken out; still it doesn't explain the madness of patrolling into the kill zone of a determined enemy. 16 Air Assault Brigade is unlike anywhere that I have served before. Tried by twelve not carried by six is echoed in every man. Hard, fast and aggressive is how they train and ultimately how they fight.

'Contact Wait Out' bellows across the net. At that moment it's 'game on' again. The net is chaotic. Du Boulay is calling for CAS (Close Air Support) and Captain Wood is all over it. Both close air and Apache pilots are hungry for targets. The platoon is danger close to munitions, but are holding their position. The Taliban stronghold is exactly that, as soon as they get eyes on the Apache they go to ground. As quick as they hide, they pop back up again and are engaging our call sign from multiple firing positions. The fire fight is relentless, our supercool JTAC calls in CAS and the sound of low flying jets gets the nod of approval from everyone in our area.

The contact goes on for some time so I start to plan for potential heat casualties. Just as I leave the ops room I hear the words 'Man down', the words are repeated several times and the news of a casualty shocks no-one. Captain Wood turns to face me and I get the usual 'you ready?' look. 'Who is it? Where are they hit?' I ask Kev to message Monty when there is lull in the fighting.'Boydy, gunshot wound to the thigh' Kev replies quickly.

The Taliban have the platoon pinned down one and a half kilometres away. In this situation a fighting withdrawal is the only option for Monty and his crew. Boydy is a big lad who will need to be carried back to Argyll. The fire fight continues and even the Apache does not subdue the insurgents housed in Shin Kalay.

After what seems like a lifetime I get eyes on the lads carrying Boydy, every man there is in turmoil. We get hands on our casualty and I am relieved to see he is still smiling. He has been shot straight through the shin and the 7.62mm round has come straight out the other side before embedding itself straight into the hamstring at the back of the same leg.

No artery has been hit, he has been lucky. The other lads are in desperate need of water, the heat has turned the one and a half kilometre casualty extraction into a marathon. Even Monty is on his arse and he is a fit soldier.

Boydy is surprisingly upbeat, after a quick assessment and treatment he is stabilised. The only thing concerning him is that he wants a cigarette. In normal circumstances I would hesitate and suggest that he shouldn't have one. His vital signs are good so I decide to let Boydy have his cigarette. Medical professionals would probably frown upon it but standing here in Nad-e Ali faced with the decision I chose not to be a medical Hitler.

Boydy was a grown adult and he knew his own body. We prepare him for transportation as we hear that the Chinook is inbound. Carrying him to the helicopter site reaffirms what the guys have just faced getting him out of contact. Shots are fired at the incoming Chinook and that sets the tone for the coming weeks. The RAF pilots aren't deterred. It would take more than a couple of rounds to stop them coming, of that I was sure. As Boydy and our dead soldier are lifted, stories begin to emerge of the events just passed. Monty tells me that Abbie carried the stretcher along with the blokes all the way back into Argyll. When I ask her about it she plays it down and jokes about Boydy's weight. She had done herself proud and looked for no recognition for it. Abbie is the sort of medic that every commander wants. She doesn't moan and is able to hold her own amongst the platoon. I was lucky to have her to rely on. My attention is suddenly switched as Monty collapses onto the floor.

He had fallen in a ditch during the withdrawal, he is in agony. His body is rigid and he is unable to bend or move. He was quite possibly the worst patient that I had to deal with. He struggled accepting help and had no plans to make life easy for us. He wanted to stay with his men no matter what. This is when you see the caliber of the infantry commanders; it supported my notion to learn from them.

After quick assessment and a couple of muscle relaxants Monty is deemed bed-ridden for at least two days. The situation down here was becoming unbearable. So many highs followed in quick succession by so many lows. It felt one big test followed by another. For now Monty was out of the game. The boss asks me if we need to replace him. I had learnt a fair amount from the physiotherapists that I had worked with in the past so I relayed to the boss that I would work on him here in the patrol base. Lt Du Boulay would have to take the platoon alone, Cpl James Henderson would step up and assume Monty's role. Hendy was an experienced section commander already so he had no problem in taking up the slack for the platoon. Mr Du Boulay was a quiet unassuming officer, he had already proved his worth amongst his men, and they had warmed to him quickly. Tonight he will move out for the first time without Monty.

A convoy is coming from Lash to re-supply us some much needed defensive stores which will help fortify this small outpost ready for the Commando Brigade to take over.

The convoy are travelling through the dark hours, a task which by now is fraught with danger. The force protection at Lash, made up of the remainder of B Company will escort the convoy to the outskirts of Nad-e Ali where they will be picked up by Lt Du Boulay and his men.

CHAPTER SIX

Patrol Base Test

We hear through briefings that foreign fighters are in the area. They are possibly fighters from Pakistan or Chechnya. This is a worrying development, these fighters have travelled some distance to be here and will no doubt be very experienced unlike the local farmers forced into battle by the Taliban. The Company's rumour control is in overdrive and we hear that further north from our location a dead insurgent was found with an Aston Villa tattoo on his body. The thought alone makes me angry. The hard facts about the Taliban's movements comes to us in intelligence reports, which are often updated every hour or even few minutes. Then there is 'rumour control' which adds ten per cent to any story.

Sunset comes and goes. For some reason there is no attack this evening and it's not long before the lads move out to meet the convoy. Jen takes her turn this time. I had got used to her working with me in the medical room, we had already dealt with our fair share of casualties and our little team worked well. I could rely on Jen to take command if I was somewhere else on the base.

As we settle in for the night the familiar sounds of panic are heard over the net. Another shocker as the Combat Logistics Patrol (CLP) heading into Nad-e Ali gets smashed by the Taliban. The lack of incoming rounds on our base was obviously saved for them and they were now limping through the desert. It was like a 'welcome to the party' Taliban style. Instead of seeing smiling, welcoming faces or locals waving flags, guests were treated to the thuds of RPG's, followed by the pleasant sound of the Dska. If a VIP was inbound then a 107mm rocket would be on hand to throw into the shit pie so tenderly prepared by the insurgency of Helmand. All this to the backdrop of small arms fire, I doze off again, still in the med room. I've learned to get sleep anywhere and anyhow I can. I knew it wouldn't be long until I was on my feet again.

Our call sign has met up with the logistics patrol, the attack on them was more of a fire power display than a full on ambush. Timing had been on our side today and it appears that the Taliban hadn't expected a road move. The convoy arrives here at Argyll in the early hours of the next morning. The lads along with Jen had been out all night. I jump up to give Davey a hand unloading the stores that have been sent, there seems to be loads and loads of kit. I'm overwhelmed by the amount of ammunition that has turned up.

The crates are endless, someone in Brigade has finally noticed that B Company are in the shit. Everyone has a little moan whilst humping the boxes off, they are so heavy. I didn't notice until today how stiff my body has become. Over a brew I listen to the stories from the guys who have driven in with the supplies. They are from 13 Air Assault Regiment, Royal Logistics Corps. They have clearly had a rough time, one soldier was hit in the helmet by an RPG which thankfully did not explode. He has to be one of the luckiest men alive. His dented helmet has since been placed in the archives of the Imperial War museum. The Jocks are humoured once more, a box has turned up full of treats. Cigarettes and cans of iron-brew, a basic requirement in any Jock diet.

Countless packets of pasta, lad's magazines in the shape of Nuts, Zoo and FHM magazines. Although tired from the long day the blokes finally had something to be happy about and for a few hours it felt like Christmas had come early. With the days starting to merge into weeks Patrol Base Argyll slowly starts to develop into a bonefide outpost. More sandbags are filled to reinforce the gun positions on the roofs. Our newly stocked rations are supplemented with tinned treats in the shape of pasta and vegetables. The Afghan soldiers make flat bread on earth fired makeshift ovens, their bread is some of the best I've tasted.

It provides the perfect accompaniment to the new ration pack main meal of chicken tikka masala. British Army rations are divided up by letter my favourite being the pack marked F. It offered steak and vegetables most evenings. Adding a bit of curry powder or tabasco sauce would offer a decent scoff. The chicken tikka menu C was new and also had the best breakfast meal. Pork sausage and beans, it was the only one that I could stomach, the rest were disgusting. Everyone was up earlier than usual to try to nab menu C before anyone else. The fresh supplies of ammunition are now being distributed to the different corners of the base; the men of B Company have continued their risky strategy of patrolling into Shin Kalay and Luis Barr.

Tonight we have more supplies coming in on a Chinook. The lift is essential as it is carrying the vital resupply of drinking water. The water that we wash with comes via a black water container (jerry can). The Afghans have found a local water source that was good enough to wash with; thankfully they also took on the responsibility of collecting it daily.

Everyone in the base is working together, Flashheart's Afghans are much more cohesive with him at the helm. He advises their Commander and so far is achieving a fair amount with the small numbers that he has left.

He continues to wear his two kneepads just as some officers insist on wearing their sweat rags like cravats. It's almost a sign of his quirkiness, if he took them off now he would get ripped up by the blokes even more. If you are going to be different then best you stick by your chosen path. I am warming to Flashheart which is a concern. It definitely doesn't have the potential to be a man-crush though.

The roads in and out of Nad-e Ali were getting worse. The convoy that delivered defensive stores just a few days ago was hit hard on its way out. Casualties were dealt with by our medical team back back at Lash. The Chinook will come in after midnight, so after last light the blokes prepare to patrol out to set up an outer cordon. This will at least stop anyone getting too close to the landing site.

Eagerly awaiting the resupply Davey and his men prepare to deploy to the HLZ, placing troops on the ground too early could potentially compromise the inbound Chinook and its crew. Within seconds of wheels up from Bastion a panicked interpreter sprints through to the Ops room.

'Sir, sir I am told the Taliban will attack a helicopter tonight.

'What the fuck!' Capt Wood putting words to all of our thoughts.

The interpreter says that ANA soldiers have been told that the local Taliban commander has a special fighter who has come into the area whose job was to attack the helicopter. He will attack before it lands.

My throat is dry as I move next door to inform Davey and Monty about what has been said. Davey hurriedly gets the QRF together and any other soldiers that are free. The Royal Irish Sgt Major Tony Mason, steps forward volunteers himself and his men from the OMLT team mentoring the Kandak to assist the effort. Tony has been manning the outgoing 51mm mortar missions along with Davey.

He has already earned the title as the calmest bloke in contact over the net. He and his small team are a very welcome addition to the base. There was no time to identify the firing point, the OC sends up all the intelligence gathered in the hope that the Chinook is called off by Brigade HQ until the morning. Surprisingly Brigade weighs up the risk and deems it safe enough for the re-supply to happen.

I wonder what on earth we will do if the airframe is shot out of the sky. The fighting platoon is already out and their cordon has covered the most probable firing points. The Kandak under control of Flashheart have also deployed out. More ground is covered now that the Kandak can be mentored.

That said the enemy were set up somewhere with full eyes on the helicopter landing site. The boss turns to me and asks if we had the capability to deal with multiple casualties should the worst happen. I reassure him that dependant on the severity of the injured we had set up other points outside the company aid post as casualty collection points, that way I could triage correctly and prioritise our patients.

I had already identified team medics within B Company and mention that I might need to use these guys to man the other clearing station for less serious injuries. He nods his head looking as reassured as he could be before considering the now difficult circumstances. The Apache gunship has arrived on station; it circles like a hawk searching for any dangers that might be visible from the sky. It's fruitless, the Apache would have to be reactive if the incident was allowed to develop. All the while the Taliban commander is, I imagine, directing the Taliban gunman who is waiting patiently in the firing point.

Everyone is on edge and nervous for the re-supply to go by without incident. We can only plan so much. Worrying about every possible eventuality would see you in an early grave for sure. The plan is in place so let's roll with what we have. If you thought about it too much you wouldn't ever leave your pit space.

I deploy out to the helicopter landing zone with Davey and sit in the dark waiting for the sound of the Chinook engines. Out of nowhere the airframe swoops in, hard and fast. The crew work like crazy to unload the water. Less than twenty three seconds down the bird suddenly lifts. I was thinking what if the 'shooter' is in position and convinced myself it was duff information. Then suddenly as the Chinook is airborne, a bright streak flashes through the darkness. A rocket has been fired and flies straight past the window of the pilot's seat. For a second I am numb.

This was quickly followed by tracer from small arms. The pilot shunts the bird forward nervously. Its huge engines lift it fast and the Chinook escapes the onslaught before flying off into the darkness. On the ground, the sound of muffled 'woo's' of relief from me and the team at the landing site are echoed as the sound is carried on the night air. 'Thank fuck for that! Ham, let's get this shite back in mucker'. Davey shouts. When we return to the ops room, the boss along with Captain Wood, are laughing like they know something we don't. It turns out the Taliban Commander has ordered the execution of the insurgent, we hear from the ANA. He had missed his target and his career was over. The insurgents still use medieval, sometimes barbaric means to achieve their aim.

Stories of how the Mujahideen treated captured Russian officers were every man's worst nightmare. Upon his return Captain Wood informs Flashheart that if he is captured he will be buggered to death by his captors. Flashheart smiles before hastily replying 'That won't be happening anytime soon Colin'.

Back to my bed space and I am sure that my roll mat is getting thinner. Only the OMLT had the sense to bring camp cots, the rest of us were sleeping rough on the floor. I try to get comfortable before being woken up again for my death radio stag. After today's incident I am out with the boss tomorrow to try and identify a secondary helicopter landing site. We will patrol into the district centre of Nad-e Ali.

I am glad to be escaping the patrol base for a couple of hours, I understand my position here and the fact that the boss needs me at a moment's notice. With no doctor my junior medics needed a haven to come back to. Experience and rank keep me in B Company's Aid Post. Patrol Base Argyll was a sitting target. The Taliban just had to fire in our general direction and they would hit something. We had already suffered one KIA here with several more injured. Events in Marjah had also taught me to be very careful what I wished for. I had developed a distinct dislike for the military tourists of this world.

Many of the foreign Commonwealth office staff in the Provincial Reconstruction Team were responsible for my dimmed view on the 'combat tourist types'.

Time after time I would see the naive civilians in flowing flowery skirts with unsuitable strappy footwear deploy out to make tourist trips to the Bolan Fair in Lash. It would serve no tactical or reconstructive purpose but it would create the perfect combat tourist photo opportunity.

This was a pet hate of mine and another subject that I would become over-efficient in voicing my opinion on. It was usually B Company providing the outer cordon security for these little jaunts.

The situation on the roads around Nad-e Ali had made any potential moves out of here impossible. It crossed my mind that flying out under the cover of darkness was the only plausible way to get me and the rest of B Company back to 'Lash Vegas'. After recent events this move was far from attractive. That 107 mm got very close and the Taliban's ability to buy surface to air missiles was never far from my mind.

As normal routine pressed on it became clear that non-battle injury and sickness was hurting us far more than the enemy. Diarrhoea of some sort was prevalent in everyone; this was often accompanied by dehydration and fatigue.

Problems involving feet became apparent as the blokes boots were sodden with water. Using the irrigation channels as cover during contact meant that many of the platoon were fighting knee deep in water. Insect bites were becoming infected and my daily sick parade was growing. I make an off the cuff remark to one of the section's second in command about the possibility of swapping Jocks on the wall and roof gun teams with soldiers in the fighting platoon. This would offer the guys suffering most to get some much needed rest. Every man was working just as hard as the next, just in different ways.

My suggestion gets back to Monty who isn't best pleased. I overhear him gripping the section's second in command for mentioning it. In hindsight I wished that I had mentioned it to Monty myself privately. My regret turns to anger when I hear Monty brief one of his blokes up for coming sick. I hear him further explain that the guys must see him prior to coming to see me in the aid post.

'Tell me that I didn't just hear that' I say to a stunned Abbie. I fly through to my medical room where Monty is resting, confronting him as I walk through the door. It reminded me of times that I would argue with my brothers and I am hoping this doesn't end the same way that they often would.

Me being stabbed in the temple with a fork or getting choked out for twenty seconds in the passage way. At home being the youngest of five was a sometimes dangerous job especially if you had a smart mouth like mine or you are the only sibling not born in Glasgow.

Monty rightfully defends the command of his platoon as I defend my suggestion to alleviate the fact that blokes are piling in daily. I tell him that from now on, he can assess all wounds coming into the aid post. 'Be sure to let me know if any fucker needs my help when their bleeding out eh, or are you going take control of our wounded from your pit space?' I say angrily. 'Get yourself te fuck Channy'. Monty hastily replies: 'Aye right' I say.

Me and Monty aren't dissimilar in character which makes for an interesting 10 minutes. B Company relies heavily on us both and the pressure is starting to show. Davey walks into the room and looks at us both he shakes his head before walking straight back out. I could see that he was disappointed that we were squabbling like two private soldiers. I head back to the command post and nothing is resolved. Everyone heard the fracas but no one comments. Slumping down onto my roll mat I remember a conversation that we had no more than a week to go. it was the same day that we had lost one of the Kandak soldiers.

Monty walked into the Company Aid Post to find the place covered in blood and myself up to my neck in shite. He had been out on patrol when the incident had happened so he had missed much of it, where I had made the difficult decision to stop my team working on the Afghan soldier. We had exhausted much of our heavily depleted medical kit.

I checked for signs of life several times to be sure that I was making the right call. Monty asked me at what point I would decide to stop working on him or one of his men. He wanted to know how long we would exhaust ourselves for. Realising that it was something that I had never thought of before, I explained to him that we weren't kitted out as well as Lash but as a team I assured him that we would keep going until they were on the helicopter and I truly meant that. Even for the sake of the morale of the troops left behind we would keep going.

Clearly if half a body or a head was missing then the un-enviable decision is made for you. Bearing this in mind I head back into the aid post. I looked at Monty knowing that we were in this shit together. He knew that as medics we would go as far as needed for him and his men and I knew that they regarded us as their own. I look at Monty trying my best to stay angry. We both start laughing.

'Sorry mate' Monty says : 'It was my fault mucker I didn't mean anything by it. I just made a passing comment that's all' I reply. We were a solid team before this, everything ran smoothly. We supported each other in everything I relied heavily on Monty to keep my medics safe out on the ground and he relied on me to keep his men alive and healthy.

The only good to come out of the argument was that we both blew off a fair amount of steam. Under the tense environment we worked in this job wasn't for the faint hearted. Our argument had emptied the aid post and I was glad that no one else chose to get involved. When you are attached to the infantry it's very easy to just turn up and make up the numbers, but my Regiment didn't deploy medics like that.

We were trained to add value; being the expert in my field I had to make sure that I never lost control of that. We were both right, our mis-communication had fucked things up as it does most things. It's like when you send a text or email and you haven't explained what you actually meant properly. When you read it back to yourself and realise that you sound like one of the crazies off the TV show 'Jeremy Kyle' you already know it's too late as you have pressed the send button. Within minutes all is forgotten but to my disgust Michael Buble is back haunting my beloved speakers.

Our biggest test was yet to come and we didn't even realise it. Just when you think that things can't possibly get worse, they do. My bed is calling me and not another word is spoken about the altercation, all I want is sleep. The night zips by and morning sees our call sign prepare to move out to recce the possible secondary helicopter landing site.

As I exchange banter with Flashheart about his dual knee pad action I retrieve my own from Mr Du Boulay. Flashheart's character lends itself to life in a patrol base. I announce that he has inspired a new test that I will perform on potential new friends or a possible future husband. I will call it the 'Patrol Base Test'. I sell the idea to Captain Wood who takes it on as his own. The test is one question followed by a yes or no answer, you can wean out the dross saving time and sometimes money.

The question is 'would I spend any length of time with this individual in a small isolated patrol base?' Flashheart passes the test; the roar of a definitive yes reverberates through the group. Our reasoning was simple firstly the double knee pad wearer, second the French coffee press, and most importantly the red iPod. Character goes a long way in the military; those who have it tend to succeed wherever they go. As we deploy out of Argyll the men of B Company seem to have found their second wind.

Jokes are shared and the blokes berate each other as the patrol steps off. It's amazing what a day's rest can do for morale. We patrol through the district centre making our way past the police station that housed us that first night. Not wanting to miss an opportunity Kev instantly reminds me of my resourceful spooning of our interpreter to keep warm on the roof.

'Good one Kev' young Ferris says and applauds his vigilance. It's hard to believe that we were ever here. That night seems like a world away, so much had happened since then. As we approach the open space that was clearly large enough to manoeuvre a Chinook, I notice that there is not a person or dog is in sight. Nad-e Ali was completely deserted. Drug paraphernalia was discarded around the floor where I was about to put my knee. I am very thankful for my kneepad.

With used needles strewn all over the shop I warn the guys behind me to be careful with the placement of their hands. We settle down in all round defence as the boss and Davey get busy, marking grids and taking photos. We don't hang about; the trip back to Argyll is far quicker than the trip out. Upon our return the Afghan Special Forces team and their mentors are busy preparing to patrol out for the first time, the entire Patrol Base is stood to, acting as a Quick Reaction Force for them.

The team deploy out and head south; within ten minutes their patrol gets whacked and is now in contact. Amidst the fire fight it emerges that two of their team were planning to kill the entire patrol including the two British soldiers who are their mentors. During the withdrawal the traitors are detained and dragged back into the base.

All is not well, dishevelled and shocked by the drama that has unfolded the Brit mentors choose to house the two in the back of separate Snatch vehicles. The boss is quickly briefed about the intent of our guests. Although operating independently on the ground, the team still came under the charge of Major Clark when housed in the PB. There was no where else to secure the two prisoners, but they had plenty of ventilation and water. Perhaps as we would discover too much ventilation.

Later that day one of the mentors asks if I could check one of the prisoners who may have sustained injuries during the initial struggle. 'No worries I will just grab my kit'. I climb up onto the roof of the vehicle so I could get eyes on through the hatch at the top. Getting in through the back door was a no go as that was now up against the solid wall at the side of the aid post. As the mentor opens the hatch and looks in, I notice a look of shock on his face. 'Gen, gen, gen, no fucking way' he says sounding completely puzzled.

For a moment I was inclined to think that the prisoner had somehow died. As I peer in I see that the back of the vehicle is empty the prisoner was missing! While I take in the magnitude of what this means I notice my yellow sharps container still sitting in its position on the side of the vehicle. We had an Afghan soldier, a Taliban sympathiser on the loose in the base. But everything was okay as my multi-purpose yellow sharps bucket was still there. The things that you think about at the most inappropriate times are often hard to comprehend.

All positions around the base are informed and everyone goes into a state of heightened alert. Every man has his weapon closer than before and movement is kept to a minimum around the base. Any complacency that may have crept in has diminished. When informed the Kandak commander goes ballistic, he demands that his men seek out the soldier that has helped with the breakout. The tension between the Afghans and Jocks has created an atmosphere of suspicion and mistrust. The base was supposed to be a safe haven for us all, well as safe as it gets in Nade-Ali anyway. The escapee is more than likely armed. With intent to kill he could wreak havoc in the camp. A widespread manhunt gets underway, every inch is searched. An hour goes by before an Afghan soldier is found harbouring the escapee.

The rapid response from Lt Col Nazim and his men leave no doubt as to where their loyalties lie. In the past few years there have been several incidents in which Afghan soldiers have turned on British and American troops. Thankfully the bond between between the ANA and the Coalition is growing as the plan to train more Afghans develops.

Someone had gotten to him to enable this situation in the first place. Orders come from higher command that the whole Afghan special forces team are to be extracted. They will be moved later tonight and won't be replaced.

The rest of the day is relatively quiet, only the fresh reports about future Taliban intentions is keeping anyone from sleeping. They are desperate to bring down a helicopter and acknowledge that they will target the next re-supply. They know that road moves are almost impossible.

We just had to ensure that the cordons were placed further out. Our helicopter wouldn't stop coming so the threat was always looming. The extraction goes by without incident and another night of unbroken sleep refreshes everyone. The following day I make use of some quiet time. I take my turn and use the satellite phone to call home. I make my way over to one of the corner positions where the signal is strongest.

Young Jock Garry Wilson is manning the .50 cal on top of the WMIK. Garry is a junior soldier, he had a tough time growing up and lost his mum at a young age. What amazes me is that he is not bitter; he lives life to the full and embraces everything. He cares for his younger brother and tries to do best by him. Soldiers like Garry make me miss home, I am always grateful for the family that I have, my Mum especially.

To lose your mum doesn't bear thinking about. I recall my friend Jenny and I talking about it one time when we were on medical placements at HMS Nelson in Portsmouth. The pair of us sat crying like muppets just thinking about it. I sit near the tailgate and proceed to make my call home, my mum answers and it's a relief to hear her voice.

Wilson suddenly gets eyes on two fighting aged males and relays the information to Scotty Pew on the roof. I get to my third or fourth sentence before the .50 cal lets rip above me. Very much aware that my mum is on the other end of the line, I hang up with haste. 'Fuck' I think as I scramble into cover and make the dash along the wall receiving incoming to get to my body armour and helmet. The rattle from the .50 cal is making my teeth chatter, it's deafening. I wished now that I hadn't called home, God only knows what my mum must be thinking.

You are forced create a normal routine, situations can go from nothing to everything so you try and make the call whenever you can. Scotty has confirmed six kills; it looked like they were setting up for an attack on us later that evening. Moving mortars and randomly engaging Wilson's position. My morale is dented in more ways than one when we find that the makeshift shower has taken some 7.62mm rounds at head height.

Everyone must now revert back to being feral – no washing again. Mega! I am desperate to call home again and to my relief all is well. Mum was happy that I was okay and I was glad that she didn't really understand what all the noise meant so I didn't tell her. I will see her in a few weeks and as resilient as mums are, I did not want her to worry any more than she had to.

CHAPTER SEVEN

Mass Casualties

The peace that morning habitually brings is interrupted by the arrival of the Throatcutter call sign. Command elements are gathering in the command post for a much needed re-group. Planning has suddenly become more focused in light of the successful completion of the turbine move to Kajaki. A switch in Brigade main effort means that the priority was now the handover of all areas of operation to 3 Commando Brigade.

Major Clark along with second in command Captain Wood are busy meticulously planning for offensive operations tomorrow. With areas surrounding Nad-e Ali becoming increasingly unstable, 16 Brigade has deployed the Pathfinder Platoon to operate in and around Marjah to our south. Small groups of Afghan SF are patrolling the desert to our north. The Kandak's main effort is to push into the areas proving to be the most problematic. In recent weeks Shin Kalay along with Luis Bah were highlighted as insurgent strongholds. Monty was back in action so he, under the command of Lt Du Boulay would reinforce the Afghans should the need arise.

The platoon would conduct low level ops just over a click away from the PB. Monty's mood is light this morning he is clearly far happier back with his men and not cooped up in the aid post. The Throatcutters would assume the role of a roving Quick Reaction Force; they would satellite the area and be on hand to provide fire support or a casualty extraction team.

These were going to be significant and dangerous operations that would probably see us through to our end of tour. The marines couldn't get here quick enough although I notice that the soldiers of B Company were more resolute than ever, this tour had already claimed the life of one member of the Regiment. He was killed by a legacy mine left here by the Russians, every man of the company was still grieving his loss. The thought of going home had motivated the jocks to finish their battle to 'hold Nad-e Ali'. Holding this ground and not allowing it to fall to the Taliban was our main effort and every soldier was committed to that mission. Flashheart was preparing for his big day out in his now customary fashion. Knee pads are pre-positioned, fresh coffee had been pressed, and Marlboro Lights were at the ready. His hair was more bouffant than normal as he pops into the Command Post for a quick shit *(pronounced shite)* chat prior to his departure. I have grown fond of his once irksome character.

The one thing that I notice about him more than most is that he doesn't take life too seriously and he has the ability to laugh at himself, he is genuine and kind hearted. I will probably read about him one day for having just won a Victoria Cross or something equally outrageous. Least to say the Kandak was more than happy to follow Flashheart into battle. Sgt Major Tony Mason of the Royal Irish will deploy alongside the Kandak, medic Gurung is assigned to the mentoring team and Sean Maloney will deploy with Monty and his crew. I will keep Abbie and Jen with me. We prepare our medical room as normal, seeing Sean and Gurung off as they leave camp.

The moment both patrols deploy a 'dicker' or spotter is located through binoculars by Scotty Pew on the roof. A spotter will often be the eyes for waiting insurgents prior to any type of attack or ambush. A good 'dicker' is usually one that is not seen. This one must have learnt his craft at the school of 'arse-clownery'. Clearly he had been skiving off or asleep during the 'covert dicker/spotter' lesson. The mass exodus of blokes allows me to tend to the small number of troops left in Argyll. I keep busy administering basic physiotherapy techniques on the increasing number of non-battle injuries in the PB. Abbie is in first complaining of uncomfortable lower back pain.

As I set about manipulating the muscles on either side of the spine, we listen to some music through the small set of speakers on the old wooden desk.

Coldplay's 'Fix You' sets the tone for what was to become for me the single worst day in Nad-e Ali. The sound of small arms ignites the radio net into action followed by the thunderous sound of the Dska. The eruption of fire power is ear-splitting, Scotty Pew has eyes on from the gun position on the roof, and it appears that the Kandak are being engaged.

Captain Wood and the JTAC get busy calling for air support in the shape of the ugly call sign. It's not long before the Apache is on station. Monty's crew are holed up in a compound, they are told to sit tight until the full picture emerges. The latest information warns of imminent attacks on both call signs, insurgents have pinpointed Monty's position. The day was going south and quick.

The Afghan Kandak are caught up in close quarter fighting, close air support waits for confirmation from the JTAC to engage targets. The sound of the hellfire missile from the Apache silences the guns for a split second, at that moment there is not a better sound anywhere on earth. The Kandak's glory is cut short as celebrations are brought to a grinding halt. Through the haze of excitement I hear a panicked voice over the net.

The muffled words 'Mass casualty' are said before a long silence. This wasn't the calm Tony Mason that I was used to. 'Mass casualty' repeated three more times. Abbie bolts upright. Jenny looks at me and I look at the floor holding my head in my hands, trying to make sense of what I was hearing. Straight through to Major Clark I feel my pulse increase and those sweaty palms are back. Captain Wood calls the Apache off before it goes in for its second run. The boss and Captain Wood are wearing the same cold and clammy look that I am. 'What's happened?' I ask. I notice when I speak that my mouth has dried up; sinking a bottle of water I hear my own gulps like they are being fired out on a loud speaker.

Major Clark announces in an exhausted, but calm voice : 'We have an incident involving possibly 12 casualties'. Tony's voice over the net announces that most of the mentoring team patrol (Brits) have been hit including my medic Gurung.

The command post is silenced, it's the pause that every commander has prior to making a workable plan. Head in hands, focusing on what needed to be done. This way of thinking is what makes the military the best in a crisis. There will be no running around like headless chickens, it is times like this when the training and preparation for deployment shows its value.

Any panic or that sort of behaviour was saved for the command tasks that civilians embark on during those 'team building' weekends in the Lake District. There will be no shouting or foaming at the mouth. This was controlled panic. You might be at thirty thousand feet and rising on the inside but on the outside you remain stalwart and typically British. I focus on my own Mass Casualty plan, and of course I had made one but would it work? The irritating but very true saying of 'no plan survives the first contact with the enemy' annoys me as I think about it. I take a few deep breaths, not big obvious sighs, just enough to ensure that my brain was actually receiving some oxygen and crack on with the task at hand. I reassure the boss that we could square this away with the medics that I had before moving next door to prepare for our inbound casualties.

I gather the two team medics of 5 Scots. LCpl Aaron Wells or 'Wellsee' and Pte Farrel Foy, these guys would deal with our walking wounded or less needy in an area just outside the aid post. Jen and Abbie would take on the more serious casualties and I would oversee the effort, getting involved only if I had to. We had set up separate casualty collection points or CCP's to house our wounded. The Throatcutters move rapidly to the Kandak's position, their task was to get our men back to the PB where we could treat them.

The boss orders Monty's platoon to finish on task and assist the stricken call sign by providing an all-round defence. That all changes within five minutes when we hear Monty screaming over the net: 'Man down... Man down!' As soon as they had left the compound the Taliban opened fire. They had waited patiently allowing the platoon to conduct their business until they were placed perfectly to be engaged. One of the lads has taken a round straight through the femur. A complicated injury at the best of times, this was news that we could do without.

'What the fuck is happening?' I say, thinking out loud. My brain is working overtime and Monty is now pinned down in the compound that they had initially occupied. I put those guys to the back of my mind. Our priority was to deal with what was coming through the door. Sean would have to work hard if the femoral artery had been hit and he was more than capable. I gather my medics and brief them on our plan of action; this is the calmest that I have ever seen them. It's a good feeling as a commander that there are no doubts in the team.

Sean was taking care of business at the point of wounding and news from the mentoring team indicated that Gurung was still managing to treat the other injured soldiers in his crew. I grab anyone who was free in the patrol base to help carry stretchers.

I am grateful that I am not short of volunteers. Brigade Headquarters back in Lash are now screaming for details of casualties. The boss will need quick and accurate information to ensure the best possible outcome for our injured. There is already one Afghan soldier confirmed KIA on the ground. The first casualties start to arrive, strewn across the tailgates of vehicles they are a sorry sight.

Two Cat Bs and one KIA so far. One by one I triage them, as I work my way through the casualties all my years of training kick in. I assign the serious head injury to Jen and the open chest wound to Abbie. The most serious are taken straight through to the company Aid Post. We receive a further four Cat C's. Wellsee and Foy set about patching them up as best they can. The mentoring team are all back in Argyll and several of them injured, Gurung my medic continues to treat the wounded, ignoring his own wounds. I have to verbally order him to stop so he can receive treatment himself. He has taken shrapnel in the legs and Sgt Maj Tony Mason has been fragged in the arms.

Flashheart has somehow managed to escape unscathed, just the sight of him gives me a much needed morale boost. He is in clip and his hair and kit are more dishevelled than ever. The wide eyed panic in his face is back.

He is again adding value at the most inappropriate time. I count up the casualties; we have 11 wounded and one man Killed in Action. Monty has yet to bring in his Cat B so that will make twelve. The boss wants a casualty report and quick. The MERT are waiting to deploy from Camp Bastion. Brigade is sending two Chinooks for the lift. I reassess all casualties ensuring that they are stable enough to fly. I confirm with the boss that we are good to go; Monty will have to meet us at the helicopter landing zone with his casualty to save time.

The overpowering midday heat makes the whole situation almost unbearable. Trying to brief people up whilst wiping sweat from your eye sockets is not without its problems. As quick as my casualty report is sent up the chain I hear that wheels are up from Bastion so there is no time to waste. Then as we try to move the injured toward the landing site.

I spot an Afghan soldier driving his truck at speed in the direction that we were now heading with our wounded. Losing any patience that I had left, I smash the butt of my rifle on the windscreen of his vehicle signalling him to stop before forcing myself inside the cab to retrieve the keys from the ignition. The other Afghan soldiers assisting us with the casualty, physically drag him from his vehicle before moving him away.

This type of Afghan madness was common place and I could not allow his stupidity to interfere with what was happening. Any loss of control could literally cost lives. Feeling like losing control was becoming a regular occurrence here; I don't know why I just got very frustrated when things didn't happen quick enough or when common sense was overlooked for stupidity. I remember always feeling like there was never enough time to make mistakes.

I was often left wondering if I was the mad one, or I was the one not making sense. This was a problem that I would have to deal with several times over when I left the military. Maybe it was my slice of PTSD (Post Traumatic Stress Disorder), who knows? I call the vehicles forward that are now laden with our wounded. Stretcher bearers follow on behind. The scene before me took my breath away. The vivid colour of blood so clear on the backdrop of desert camouflage. I could see people mouthing words but I couldn't hear a thing. We had casualties that were physically hurt but we also had young men in shock and would need attention. We would have to deal with them later when the carnage was cleared. Moving slowly towards the landing zone, I give Abbie one set of handover notes and I take the other. The four Cat B's are split and the remaining Cat C's will be divided equally between the airframes.

Sean and Monty suddenly appear at the front gate with Pte Gordan Coakse or 'Coaksee'. His eyes are rolling in the back of his head, and he is barely conscious. The casualty extraction from the compound had taken its toll. I couldn't risk keeping him here so he would be evacuated along with the rest.

Sean administers quick interventions and monitors Coaksee until the lift. As we settle the casualties down in the usual position to the side of the landing site, without warning one of the Afghan soldiers decides to walk straight across the LZ. A Chinook is literally hovering above him, coming in to land. By some miracle the downdraft disorientated him enough to move him towards my position. I try to remain calm wondering how someone could be so foolish.

My patience again is short-lived. I grab him by the collar on his uniform forcing him face first into the dirt. I nursed a vision of him losing his head to the low rotor blades at the front of the Chinook; if I am honest I almost wished that he had for being so utterly reckless in such a desperate time. There is never an explanation for the Afghan madness that I witness, no one is ever held accountable. These days are reminding me of the film 'Tropic Thunder' in which Robert Downey Jr's character said it was uncool to go 'Full retard' or completely off the wall.

It seemed that between them, Medi the Afghan who fired the RPG, the driver from earlier and the potential Chinook suicide that several people had gone 'Full retard'. Both Chinooks land simultaneously; the familiar faces on the back of the airframe were a welcome sight. Doctors from my regiment handed us bags full of medical kit and goodies from the NAAFI shop.

The casualties go on and this time the Afghans get it right, they control themselves and for a moment I am proud of the medical section that we had been mentoring. I recall the day that I had to confiscate a ton of narcotics and controlled substances from them; they had been feeding RPG man Medi diazepam for his 'all over Afghan body pain'. His inaccuracy with the RPG in the early days was probably a direct result of the fact that he was wasted. Much had changed since then and we had forged a great working relationship with our Afghan medical counterparts.

As casualties were systematically handed over our team move off and take cover from the downdraft. The two Chinooks lift off the ground together. It was incredible, the buzz from adrenaline was like nothing that I had felt before. It wasn't until the dust settled and the sound of the engines petered out in the distance that I wished that I was on one of those birds and heading home.

Running back to the patrol base, Monty tells me that Coaksee had been part of the casualty extraction team. His body had suffered for it. Heat injury will kill someone quickly, but Coaksee was in the capable hands of the MERT team now and we would have to wait a few hours for news on any of our casualties.

The aid post is in chaos, I don't know where to start. Blood covers much of our equipment and the sodden clothing from casualties including their shoes are still placed where their bodies had lay. Vomit covered the floor where Jenny had dealt with the head injury. Of all our patients I was most doubtful for his recovery. I needed some water and fast, bottles get passed around the team. No one speaks for ten minutes or so, silently taking in the magnitude of what had just happened. As stories emerge about the cause of the carnage out there today, relief changes to anger and It soon becomes clear why. Our guys weren't shot up by a well dug in Taliban position nor had they encountered a daisy chain of IEDs as first thought. They had been hit by the Apache gunship hellfire missile, or fragmentation from it, the same hellfire that we were celebrating hours earlier. No-one took the news calmly, least of all Davey and the boss. After a tense time in the command post it transpired that friendly grids given over the net were mis-communicated as enemy grids.

The Apache pilot wasn't at fault, he was engaging what he thought were enemy positions. Luckily Captain Wood called the Apache off just before he was going in for a second run; the second in command's quick reaction stopped the Apache re-engaging. No one wants to take responsibility for such a colossal fuck up. All patrol commanders thrash it out in the Ops room leaving relations between B Company and the Throatcutters strained to say the least. No one was talking and I could see that the command post was enraged. The truth of the matter was it was down to age old 'fog of war' miscommunication, it's never ideal but it does happen.

The base was on its knees when it came to manpower. The Company needed battlefield replacements. With Sgt Major Tony Mason from the mentoring team out of the game, Davey needed a number two for any outgoing 51 mm mortar missions. I offered my assistance and he accepted. Tony is a Royal Irish Regiment soldier and had been injured in an attack and airlifted to Camp Bastion. Now with a man short in fact the entire base was short of manpower and someone was needed to help defend the base. I was to fill the role of Number Two on the 51 mm mortar. Times had now become desperate and it was a case of everyone doing whatever they could to help and ensure that our mission to hold Nad-e Ali didn't fail.

As a combat medic the military's Law of Armed Conflict states that I can only fire in anger in order to protect myself and or my casualties, unless the circumstances were deemed exceptional. With 66 out of 100 soldiers injured and four Afghans soldiers dead Nad-e Ali was now in exceptional circumstances. I thought about us being over run and slaughtered by the Taliban and the potential repercussions. I speculated that the newspapers would have a field day with comments such as 'female medic among the dead, because she refused to man the mortar'. You are always going to be wrong whatever you deem is right, weak if I die while surrounded by munitions and wrong if I choose to survive and use them.

After the death of my brother David I knew that I would never allow myself to become a victim and if there was a chance that I could do something or anything to avoid that, then I would do whatever was necessary. As the temporary Number Two on the mortar my role was to prime or arm mortar rounds for Davey. Ironically, I had been trained how to use the weapon at the Infantry Training Centre in Brecon, but never fired it. It is a small weapon and easily man-packable and it was often used when the Taliban attacked at night. The team would fire what is called 'para-illum', a non-lethal shell which at a fixed height detonates and lights up the night sky.

Its powerful flare lasts for almost 30 seconds and allows the Jocks to identify the location of enemy fighters hiding under the cover of darkness.

There was a time that this would have been unheard of - a female helping out. Blokes down here weren't bothered anymore. It didn't matter what cap badge you were so long as you could do the job. The days of definitive front lines were over, this was a 360^{0} battlefield. Marjah had already proved that, in my opinion every soldier must be prepared or at least be capable of reacting. I was grateful for the hideous training that I had put myself through prior to this deployment.

It made me comfortable enough to volunteer for roles outside of my usual skill set. I spent much time with Scotty, a Sgt in 2 Para's Support Company, learning about support weapons prior to my basic tactics and senior range qualification courses down at the Infantry Training Centre Brecon. I was grateful that he took the time to teach me. He must have got something right as I was about to embark on my first mortar mission. It was a hesitant one. I knew its capabilities, but had never fired it. I had to learn fast. Davey fired, I handed him mortars from the crate making sure that the safety pin was pulled off the side of the nose fuse as that's the way that you arm the bombs before firing them.

We worked well together and I got to practice firing when using the illuminated flares or smoke rounds, this would ensure that I got it right before firing any of the high explosive or HE rounds. We go through several crates before coming across a crate of duff mortar rounds. The short time I spent on the 51 mm took my mind off the depressing reality of how many casualties we were taking. The company aid post was always my first priority but this secondary task gave me something other than blood to focus on. I recall one particular scenario when I regretted my decision to help. Patrol Base Argyll was under attack, Davey and I hurried out to our mortar line.

Straight into it. Major Clark asked for: 'Five rounds from the 51, fire for effect Sergeant Major' off we went like a well-oiled machine. Within seconds the boss sprinted out of the command post screaming for us to take cover. Intelligence had identified incoming IDF was imminent.

Me and Davey lay face down in the dirt waiting for the incoming mortars to land. We were out in the open ground in no cover at all. Sheltered by my mark 6 alpha helmet and the plates from my Osprey body armour. I think back to that moment and found myself thinking. 'What the fuck was I thinking volunteering? Hadn't I learnt anything?'

There by the grace of God went I and Davey. I had a lot of admiration for Davey, mainly because he cared so much for his men. Their welfare was his priority and he made sure that they knew it. He was the bearer of all news good or bad. Later that evening he summoned me to the command post informing me that one of my own section medics has been shot down in the Nawa district south of Lashkar Gah. We had been there the week before this mayhem had started. LCpl Andy James was evacuated to Camp Bastion and was on his way home. The news put the whole team on a downer; the days were bringing nothing but bad news. Andy was due to join us down here in Nad-e Ali. It could be worse though, at least he was alive. I retire to my roll mat for some much needed quiet time.

A quick hour should do the trick. Closing my eyes I fall into the deepest sleep. Ten minutes in and the patrol base is hit again. 'For fucks sake' I mutter as I wake like a bear with a sore head, body armour and helmet straight on. Rounds ping their way through the ops room windows this time. Ricocheting around the room, a young Jock narrowly missed yells out: 'Ah well, better luck next time, ya fuckin bawbags'. This puts a smile on my face, adding value at the worst possible time I thought. Flashheart is up and about clutching his red iPod.

'You alright Sir?' I ask politely lying back on my roll mat 'I'm always alright Sgt T' he smiles 'red iPod okay?' I say. No reply this time, just an awkward smile followed by an awkward silence. Captain Wood laughs in the corner before mumbling the words 'man crush' under his breath. The humour that is passed around is what keeps everyone going. If it weren't for the soldiers of B Company, I would have wished my way onto a helicopter a long time ago. After a truly desperate couple of days, I wonder what may become of us. We are now down to two platoons of men, they aren't fully manned and no OMLT to mentor the worn out Kandak.

We have lost four soldiers so far and should count ourselves lucky that there haven't been more. We have another no-patrol day, the news is most welcome. I can finally get some personal administration done. Flashheart and his now ineffective team await the arrival of the new OMLT and B Company awaits the arrival of the first elements of 42 Commando. The Kandak will remain in place until further notice, not a nice prospect to face but they carry on regardless. I remember meeting the OC, Officer Commanding L Company who would be replacing us in Lash. He was on his advance reconnaissance package quite some time ago. Recces seem to be done way too early by us Brits; a lot can change in just a few days or weeks.

Then by the time you turn up your area of operations is completely different to what you briefed your blokes back home. Major Clark took him on a familiarization patrol around Lash District Centre. It was the day we encountered a male suicide bomber dressed in a burqa. Luckily the Afghan Police shot him dead before he could detonate near Governor Gulab Mangal's compound. I noted that the Burqa he was wearing was bright pink. He was also struggling in feminine, glitter - emblazoned heels. Not the low profile suicide bomber that I had expected. The L Company commander would be bringing his men straight into Nad-e Ali, they were in for an interesting start to their tour.

CHAPTER EIGHT

Ali Cat

The advance party of Royal Marines are inbound this morning; my first thought is how disappointed they might be when they realise that the base's shower is out of bounds. I had served alongside members of 42 Commando in Sierra Leone, they provided our small reconstruction team with force protection when we deployed to the more austere areas up country.

The Royal Marines were definitely a different breed. My grandfather was a Royal who fought in Korea. 'Buck Taylor' was part of 'The Raiders' 41 Independent Commando. His unit suffered great losses. When he talked of his time in Korea he spoke quietly of the day they had deployed on a daylight raid into the area of Sonjin, many of his close friends never made it home. 41 Independent Commando were awarded an American Presidential Unit Citation in 1957. Extremely proud of his days as a Commando he was buried in his much loved Green Beret; his regimental blazer was rarely off his back. He died in 1999 aged 74. I was serving on Operations in Kosovo at the time. I received a letter from him, he must have written it before he died.

I would read it time and time again. I liked the way that he wrote; it was old fashioned and our handwriting was exactly the same. In his letter he told me to trust no man and never turn my back on the enemy. He went on to quote 'The Man in the Arena' a speech given by then American President Theodore Roosevelt in 1910. The junior medic in me had no real understanding of what any of it meant.

Afghanistan was where the penny finally dropped. Neither a grunt nor a man, a soldier serving in support of a Brigade made up of the type of men that he was talking about. The speech was about men like him, men who put themselves out there, men who pushed themselves and weren't afraid of the prospect of failure. With all the action in Nad-e Ali came plenty of quiet time, often tending thoughts of family and close friends and how much they meant to me. I was extremely proud of my grandfather and never got the chance to tell him. They don't make them like him anymore, he didn't blame an ex-wife or husband or poor upbringing for the few issues that he had. Nowadays people don't want to take any responsibility. It always has to be someone else's fault. I look at my own faults and like most people I have plenty. For the most part though, they make me who I am. It took me a while to take responsibility for being impatient, sometimes unwavering.

When he spoke about trusting no man or not turning my back on the enemy, I smiled thinking, when will I ever be face to face with the enemy? Maybe Marjah was what he was talking about. I hadn't planned to engage or kill anyone that day, sometimes you are forced into the 'arena' whether you like it or not. It's the action you take that will often decide your fate; an element of luck can be useful at times too.

I wondered why us, the Coalition had been so trusting; sometimes there's no choice. Both we Brits and Americans had been hit hard by supposedly trusted Afghans who in some cases had worked alongside them for many years. I think that this was the type of enemy that my grandfather was talking about.

The Commandos have their own quirks that seem almost ritualistic, like their shower fetish. Wake up, shower, go for a run, shower, have a lunch time nap, possible shower to refresh, afternoon gym session, shower and bedtime? Shower. That certainly wouldn't be the case here, water at a premium the grunts and attached arms usually opt for the much loved '3 Para shower' which meant clean nothing or do the bare minimum. Support elements from the incoming unit will be first to arrive; it's unclear how the main body will arrive. According to the boss, a move by air was the most probable.

We will hand over our vehicles and equipment just the same as we would have back in the PRT compound. It seems cooler today, the majority of the guys on the base taking a well-earned rest. Abbie and I sit chatting outside the company aid post with a cup of tea, enjoying some biscuits fruit. The military sometimes describe things in a backward fashion. Anyone normal would say 'fruit biscuits'. They weren't dissimilar to the old school Garibaldi biscuits, the ones that your dad normally likes, right up there with Jamaica cake or corned beef. The Army version was never as nice as the real McCoy they were Tesco value biscuits fruit as opposed to Tesco's finest.

Jen and Sean are sleeping when Abbie spots something moving about underneath the WMIK sitting directly in front of us. She climbs underneath to see what it is. 'It's a kitten!' she says in a surprised voice.

The little thing had been foraging in a discarded ration box, probably looking for food. She manages to lift the animal out from its shelter. I was brought up around dogs and much preferred their company. Kosovo was the first time that I had any type of association with cats. We adopted a tiny black and white kitten; he would often sleep on my camp cot while I was out. Although independent, he would show loyalty to those who he thought had earned it.

I had gotten used to him and quite liked his attitude. Unfortunately 'Scooby' was put down by an overzealous environmental health technician. I didn't show it at the time but I was secretly gutted and if I am honest a bit angry that the little man had been killed, he was a welcome distraction and didn't harm anyone. On a more professional note he kept the mice and rats at bay around the tented camp.

Soldiers are well known for their kindness to animals, especially looking after dogs and cats on operations. They provide a source of normality in what are very abnormal circumstances. So long as you don't start cutting about like Dr Doolittle then I saw no harm in keeping animals around camp. Common sense says that you can't have wild packs of dogs running around a base or snakes climbing over camp cots like something out of the 'Jungle Book'. Presuming he is a male, Abbie gives him some water, after all this time we finally find a worthwhile purpose for our army ration pate. The kitten loved it and it meant that I had found a bonefide reason not to eat it. It sounded more professional than my usual 'it tastes like shite' excuse. We named him Ali Cat on account that he had survived Nad-e Ali and this was an 'ally' achievement for a kitten. 'Ally' is a word generated from The Parachute Regiment and has a number of connotations.

Ally in Regt terminology means effortlessly looking the part. 'Ally' kit, refers to having and wearing clothing which look different to every one else. A classic example was when the paras first went into Helmand they wore different helmet covers to everyone else, which were 'ally' and quickly adopted by all units. The word is also used in general context to describe a brave or outstanding act.

Ali Cat became a permanent fixture in and around the ops room, much to the disapproval of the boss. Ali Cat even forced Davey to show his compassionate side. We would often find the Sgt Major playing with or feeding him. Just the previous week Davey had unintentionally traumatized himself with an incident involving another cat in the Patrol Base. Ham had found a kitten, it was far smaller than Ali Cat, smaller than my hand in fact; you could only just make out its features. Initially the main effort was to find its mum, every inch of the base was searched, gun positions, toilet block but there was no sight of her. I found it strange that a nursing mum would go so far away from a new born. But maybe this was the way that cats rolled in Afghanistan. All of a sudden everyone on camp became an expert in 'wild cat behavior'. I had again become proficient in how to be 'feral' if that was any use. The overall consensus was that she wasn't coming back.

Bearing this in mind we tried to nurse the kitten ourselves. The culturally different Afghans wondered why we were all so bothered. It's just a cat after all. I didn't realise until I looked back, that with so much destruction around them the blokes often needed an outlet to show kindness to. This would help mend the mental scarring that in some would be inevitable. We might not have realised it but these small slices of normality were what made us different to our enemy.

The Jocks wouldn't hesitate to push a bayonet into another human being but they would show compassion and kindness to a sick dog without thinking about it. Usually it's the children of war that soldiers reach out to; their innocence can sometimes uplift the desperate and unforgiving reality of battle. There were no kids in Nad-e Ali and we were using their school as a patrol base. The Jocks won't act like they are bothered by the circumstances but during quiet times showing some affection to a small kitten wasn't so uncool and it gave them something other than killing the Taliban to think about. Our efforts to feed the new born were fruitless and it was cruel to leave it to die in the heat. We tried everything, even making some milk out of the powder in the sachets that we are issued in our ration packs. After much discussion about its fate, we agreed that the best thing for everyone was to put it out of its misery.

Listing ways to kill the kitten humanely took some time; Jocks can be very creative when they want to be. The subject of drowning was thrown in, my least favourite way to die. Initially not so keen I couldn't come up with a better solution myself so death by drowning was the chosen method. My own refusal to die by drowning came from an incident that happened way back when I was five years old enjoying a holiday to Miami with my family. Dad had a small win on the football pools coupon. It was 1981; the same year that Charles and Diana married we watched it in our hotel room. On one occasion we took a day trip to a huge water park. 'Wet 'n' Wild', doesn't sound too child friendly to me when I read the name back to myself now, maybe I have become too cynical.

Being the youngest of five, I didn't like anyone doing more than me, constantly pushing myself too far. The incident was me all over, biting off far more than my insolent mouth could chew but still managing somehow to scrape through it. As most new swimmers do, I decided to follow my older siblings down one of the larger water slides. My dad, who I get my sense of invincibility from happily placed me front-facing on a mat before asking.

'Are you ready Channy?'

'Yes Dad' I replied beaming from ear to ear.

Off I went, speed ever increasing and my small frame started to spin out of control eventually losing my comfortable mat. My carefree smile quickly turned to a fretful look of panic. My mum was waiting at the bottom of the slide for my older brothers and sister. She didn't expect me to be on the slide with the pool at the bottom being so deep. To her horror she got eyes on me flying head first above the water line before face planting into the deep end of the pool. Struggling to breathe from the trip down the slide I gasped for oxygen before going under the water. It's that initial panic that I dread. I am a strong swimmer now having no fear of water, I just wouldn't like to be starved of oxygen too often.

Who was going to take on the task of drowning the new born? Nobody stepped forward; the hard Scotsmen facing the Taliban did not want any part in killing a kitten. In the end it was left to B Company Sgt Major Davey, an undertaking that he looked upon through less than eager eyes.

I knew that he didn't want to do it and the whole situation got worse when he asked for the use of my multi-purpose yellow sharps container. 'No way Davey' I half joked, this was the only life support that I had. I used it for everything so this had to be a definitive no go. The vision of a dead kitten whilst washing my smalls was the last thing that I needed.

Davey found a container and made sure that the water was of a decent temperature. Why? I don't know, but it made him feel better. As he set about his mission we figured that it would take two minutes maximum. Just like I thought though, the easy death by drowning method was nonsense. It's neither quick nor painless. Davey was stuck there for over seven minutes, two hands on the new born; no-one could believe it. When the Sgt Major finally re-appeared he was quieter than normal, I felt sorry for him. Not the young Jocks though, they were already planning from which angle to mock.

Later that evening the traumatic events of drowning the new born took on an even more sinister turn. The kitten's mother returned. 'Jesus fuckin Christ, no way' I hear Davey shout from next door. Her cries were agonisingly loud. It woke the entire patrol base; she positioned herself outside the aid post where Davey was sleeping. She stayed for hours; she must have sensed that the kitten had been in there. The following morning chants of 'cat killer' and 'moggy murderer' were banded about the command post. That's how people get through these insufferable situations; usually laughing at someone else's suffering or mocking someone's fuck up. It didn't matter what rank you were either, everyone was fair game. The Jocks on the wall were laughing at the irony of it all.

Davey had honourably stepped forward to do the right thing as most Sgt Majors do. In doing so he had put himself and the kitten's mother through emotional trauma. In this game you have to learn to see the funny side, if you didn't you would end up consumed with the sometimes hopelessness of it all.

The Jocks are always sure not to go too far with Davey; good to his blokes he might be, a figure of fun he is not. I hear him mention to Ferris that the container that he used for the kitten would take his head 'ne dramas' should the need arise. The deed was done, on the plus side though and as a direct result of the death by drowning incident Ali Cat got a lot more attention and became Davey's new mucker.

As the Jocks continued to probe Shin Kalay, their daily jaunts were becoming more perilous than ever. Firmly into routine the base soaked up the daily attacks. Myself and Davey continued to defend the lads with use of the 51 mm mortar when we came under attack. Scotty Pew's gun team on the roof were our lifeline, he directed us on the mortar, monitoring Davey's fall of shot. Any doubts that I had about helping out had all but faded. But thankfully my role was temporary. Every man in the Patrol Base now had a task, my medics supported every operation that happened whether inside or outside of the Base.

Just when it seemed that our luck was turning B Company faced a further blow. The boss announces that Monty would be going back to the reconstruction team base to brief the incoming marines on what to expect when they get here. It was absolutely necessary, but that didn't make it any easier for the base losing him. He would be replaced at some stage by Sgt Damian Partridge, Damo had already been bloodied this tour but until his arrival Lt Du Boulay would lead the fighting platoon alone. The men of the fighting platoon were battle weary. The young section commanders had aged well beyond their years. The experience that these soldiers had accumulated was far more than any course could teach them.

I wondered where they would go from here. For them It didn't get any better than this, other operations would surely pale into insignificance. New faces were arriving; they would stay here through the winter. No one in our Brigade really appreciated just how unforgiving this place would become. No new medics as yet, we were told that they would be arriving with the main body and this time they would be deploying a doctor down here. 'Better late than never' I grumble to Kev. With the incoming marines jokes had already started about the language barrier between the jocks and anything other than army slang.

The Royals would be enjoying their food or 'scran' as opposed to 'scoff' and a cup of tea was a 'wet' and not a 'brew'. The Jocks were rough and ready, their welcoming nature always meant that they were open to new ideas as Ferris explained.

'I dunni give a fuck who's takin over, just get them here'. That was his take on the handover and it was echoed throughout the Company. He had such a beautiful way with words. The young Jocks lust for life was infectious. They had nothing to prove to anyone, at their worst they were probably at their best. 'If you are hangin oot yer arse, then at least have the decency to do it with panache eh?' sentiments echoed from Ham. He was still cutting about on his quad bike and trailer.

A message comes through from my higher echelon at Camp Bastion. Jenny and I would be leaving sooner than we thought, we would be moving a few days before Abbie and Sean. We were already booked on flights home, no one wants to be the first to leave but orders are orders and not requests. Our exit should be at least a few days away yet so packing up wasn't starting any time soon. I didn't want to tempt fate and pack too early. Having said that I didn't have too much kit here, just enough to make my bergen uncomfortably heavy for the helicopter ride back to the Main Operating Base at Lash.

The Company's second in command was on the same flight as us. He too was required to work with the marines during the hand-over phase. The boss wasn't over enthused that we were leaving; he tried in vain to keep us all until the bitter end. Everyone trusted each other and that had taken a fair amount of time to build.

Captain Wood had made his mark down here; he'd saved the lives of countless soldiers. As the now uninteresting dusk attack came to an end I made my way back into the aid post after manning the 51 mm with Davey. I had gotten so used to the sounds of munitions that I was often tempted just to sack off taking cover. Complacency is often hard to fight. Thankfully that's the time when personal discipline has to kick in. Rounds were freely pinging around this base at all times of day.

Taking off my soaking wet body armour I notice the boss at the door with a dejected look on his face.

'Sgt T, can I have a word?' He says.

'No worries Sir, I will just be a second'.

I was nervous, I had seen that look before and I knew that bad news was about to follow. I automatically thought about family members and dreaded what he was about to say.

'It's Ham' he says. Confused I followed the boss outside. He took me around the side of the ops room so we were out of earshot of the young Jocks.

'Ham has received some bad news from home, it's his wife' explained the boss. It turns out that Ham was needed at home and things were moving fast. With any type of family sickness the military will pull out all the stops to get the affected soldier home. I find Ham sitting near the back wall outside the aid post. We were great mates, putting my arms on his shoulders I pressed down tightly. Ham was like a brother to me, I felt choked for him. It's the worst feeling in the world. It's hard to watch someone suffering especially him usually being the constant source of amusement.

He had a long journey ahead of him. The situation brought to mind my long trip home from Cyprus. I had been on exercise when I received a phone call about my brother's condition. I got back to the UK in time to turn Dave's life support machine off. Ham would be flying from Nad-e Ali to Bastion, Bastion to Kandahar and then onto Kabul. His flight from Kabul was the long stretch that worried me. If we had a doctor in Nad-e Ali then they could take care of it. I placed one tablet in a dispensing envelope and gave it to Ham explaining that it would help him sleep on the final and longest leg of his journey. I wrote a small prescriptive note that Ham could hand to anyone if required. It wasn't normal practice but these weren't normal circumstances, I had decided to take the hit should anything come of it.

Heading back into the medical room, I look around at our mediocre setup wondering how we had gotten through the last seven weeks. Suddenly the OC reappears in the doorway. 'Sgt T, the flight has been brought forward on account of Ham's situation so you, LCpl Young and the second in command will be leaving Nad-e Ali in a few hours.'

That moment seemed to change things for me, I felt freaked out at the thought of leaving. I knew where I stood down here I had a job to do. My team was fully committed to this company. We had our routine good or bad and it worked. I felt awkward at the thought of going back to Lash and couldn't understand why. It was the same type of dread that you have when you are starting a new job. I was apprehensive about going back to normality. 'We had better pack Jen' I say breaking the silence. Jen travelled light; out of all our team her personal administration was by far the best. Everything had its place; she didn't care much for niceties. It wasn't easy leaving Abbie or Sean but that's just the way it has to be sometimes. We couldn't stay in Nad-e Ali forever. After an hour our packing was done. Bergens were moved outside the aid post onto the small pathway leading to the front gate. With the little time that we had left I make my way around the base to say goodbye to the Jocks on the wall.

I get eyes on young Ferris and Cameron, two junior Jocks who I had known since their days as young recruits. Cam was a recruit in my platoon. I hand any spare kit out I have, the gun position at the front gate gets my beloved speakers so they can enjoy music during the quiet times of the day. As the four of us prepare to make our way out to the landing zone for the last time, the threat on our birds comes to the forefront of my mind. B Company commander shakes all of our hands before we set off. I always find that part a bit embarrassing, we Brits don't deal with accepting or giving praise very well. Doing a good job is what's expected.

It's dark now, picking up my things I get eyes on Ali Cat, I want to smuggle him home with me. Picking the little man up for the last time was harder than I imagined. Looking back now I realise that getting attached to anything was something that I struggled with, it freaked me out; I put much of my inability to want to get emotionally involved down to not dealing with Dave's death properly. No one ever thinks it's going to happen to them, I remember feeling guilty for wishing that it was someone else's brother that had died. No one comes away unscathed, it took some time to recognise my grief and in the end I had to try not to be so hard on myself. No replacements are in tonight, they will arrive tomorrow.

Davey leads us out to the landing zone, the straps from my back pack dig deep into my now scrawny frame. The Helmand diet is the best kept secret in the world. Wheels are up from Bastion. Kneeling in complete darkness, we listen for the sound of the Chinook, wondering if the Taliban will hit this time. I do well to try and think of something else. The bird is inbound, the four of us shelter each other as it comes in, as always the heat from the downdraft makes it hard to breathe. One by one like pensioners we clamber up with our heavy kit making our way onto the back of the Chinook.

I go on last and don't have a place to sit. I kneel with my heavy pack still on my back thinking that it's only going to be a short trip. I grab Jen's arm as we take off, unsure why it just felt like the right thing to do. Every man was aware that it was only a matter of time before one of our birds is shot out of the sky. Half an hour later the ramp is lowered on the back, we are at Camp Bastion to drop Ham off. As he passes me I stick my hand out. He taps it on his way past, giving me the 'catch you later' nod. The helicopter lifts again; I grab hold of a metal box to steady myself. My right leg has gone numb; the thought that it will fail me when I need to stand up consumes my time. Almost there now I think, as the contents of my stomach leaping up as the helicopter drops low and fast.

The pilots' aim is to evade potential rocket attacks, skimming roofs of compounds on the approach to the reconstruction team at Lashkar Gah is like a roller coaster ride at night. The door gunner standing to the rear of the airframe lifts his night vision goggles and taps my shoulder. As I look up he points to his watch and gestures two fingers, indicating that we will be on the ground in two minutes. I pass the info to Jen who in turn passes it on to the next man.

Finally wheels are down. On the ground the aircraft sits behind a high perimeter wall giving it some degree of protection, pilots are anxious to lift again as staying put for any length of time increases the chance of attack tenfold. All pax are ushered off, my dead leg is slow to react as I manoeuvre myself up. The change in engine pitch signifies the lift, taking cover I instruct the civilian that had joined us from Bastion to face away from the bird. A face full of shingle style pebbles would not have ended the day well. He worked for the Foreign Commonwealth Office, another jobs worth whose lack of understanding was encouraging our mission to fail. The shadow of the Chinook disappears into the night sky. Our medical team are waiting for us Doc Richards along with Stevie Housden had waited up for us. My brain was still in patrol base mode, I felt overwhelmed by the noise of the reconstruction team's compound.

At night Argyll was often silent unless we were under attack, the sound of generators and the glare from the perimeter lights made me feel uncomfortable. I thought about Ham and how he would be feeling. Jen and I drop our kit off in the 9 x 9 canvas shelter that we had left seven weeks prior. I head to the internet cabin as it's late so the terminals must be free, Jen heads to the shower block. To my delight the internet is down, grumbling with discord I make my way back to my camp cot. Just as I am about to climb through the small flap of canvas I hear a loud Scottish voice. 'Hey Hey Mucker.'

Turning I see a figure moving very quickly towards me. Out of the shadow I see it's my man Duffy. He lifts me off the ground, his smiling face lights up. It's young soldiers like Duffy that make this war worthwhile. They don't fight for political gain or to hunt terror cells they fight for each other in the hope that they all make it home. Our so called 'Playstation Generation' fight hard in Helmand and continue to do so. For that moment, I was glad to have left Nad-e Ali.

CHAPTER NINE

Homeward Bound

Returning back to Lashkar Gah, tired and dishevelled as I look down at my camp cot for the first time in seven weeks. Not as comfortable as my bed at home but a world away from the thin roll mat I had left behind on the floor of the Patrol Base. I was exhausted, so drained that I completely sacked off any notion of a shower, the last thing I wanted was to feel refreshed or wake myself up. Trudging over to the toilet block with my toothbrush in hand, I make short work of an essential strip wash managing to get back to my bed space within five minutes. I didn't care about anything other than getting a good nights sleep.

My body's natural adrenaline from the daily attacks and copious amounts of casualties had kept me going in Nad-e Ali; but now I felt like a zombie, the walking dead. Before Jen has chance to put the light out I am flat out and comatose. It's the deepest sleep that I have ever had, not stirring I manage a straight twelve hours. If I could bottle it and sell it as a sleep aid, I would make millions. Waking up was a different story though a major hangover headache, minus the alcohol.

I was completely dehydrated, hungry, dying for the toilet and not a multi-purpose yellow sharps container in sight. Trekking out to the toilets I get eyes on myself in the mirror, hideous I think, looking at the huge dark circles around my usually smiling Irish eyes. My skin felt like a leather belt to touch and I looked completely weather beaten. I figure that I had lost about 25 lbs in weight and I now resembled Tom Hanks' character in the film 'Castaway', the only thing missing being the beard. The fact that my combats were hanging off my arse was an unusually welcome sight.

I was enjoying the emptiness of the shower block; using a toilet without the worry of the murder hole at head height had all of a sudden become a significant event in my life. Here I was still in Helmand province but I felt safe for the first time in weeks; Nad-e Ali was raw and untamed, a world away from the reconstruction team in Lash. It took an absolute age to scrub myself clean. The grime was embedded all over me. I stayed in the shower for over an hour, trying to zone out and get back to reality. I kept thinking about Abbie and Sean. Ali Cat would be wondering where I had gone, I had gotten used to him sleeping on my doss bag at night, I liked the sensation of his little paws climbing over me to get comfy, he would try to move stealthy, stalking shadows in the room before tumbling over.

Jen and I finally get into a clean set of combats; she starts packing as I endeavour to find out information about flights home. The PRT was filling up with 3 Commando Brigade staff. Barely recognising people as I passed them along the walkways, just outside the regimental Aid Post I spot Captain Wood and he looks as dishevelled as me. 'Sleep well? When are you headed to Bastion?' he asks.

'Too well' I reply adding 'Just waiting for timings. We are out tomorrow morning, then moving to Cyprus a couple of days after that'.

'Come up to the Ops room before you leave, Monty is briefing the Marines up and Flashheart is still cutting about'.

'Thanks, and I will.' Double knee pads pop into my head as I continue to walk along the stone path to the clinic. Chuckling to myself at the thought of Flashheart and his activities around the base I make my way into the medical reception. Major Richards our Doc informs me that we are moving to Bastion after first light tomorrow morning. With no time to spare I look forward to another few hours of packing. Walking around Lash I felt empty; I went to B Company Ops Room just to be around the guys that I had been with in Argyll. Ham had made it back home in less than 24 hours so the day was already looking brighter.

I was in danger of becoming one of those mincers, the kind who excuses their poor behaviour by blaming it all on the terrible things that they have seen on operations. That wasn't me at all so from that moment on I decided to man up and start cutting about the place. I had left Nad-e Ali that was someone elses responsibility now.

A trip to the Quarter Master's Department brought me straight back to reality. Handing in kit that I had signed for turned into an epic, watching staff finish off games of solitaire before signing me off, soon raised the issue of my unwavering impatience. Its return signified that I was getting back to normal. Seeing Flashheart and his red iPod one last time sent me into a laughing fit. My stomach hurt, I was laughing so hard. Flash was still adding value at inappropriate times. Marines in the ops room looked at him in disbelief; they didn't get the joke about the red iPod either. Coffee press in hand we headed for lunch.

My new sense of purpose made the day race by; I wanted to get to Bastion so I could catch up with friends that had been deployed to different areas up country. I could also get an update on Abbie and Sean. I finish packing; say my good byes and head to my crappy tent for the last night. My head hits the pillow early for another awesome night's sleep. Just before first light, myself and Jen make our way to the landing zone.

It's busy with people waiting to fly to Camp Bastion, as the bird swoops in kit and equipment is placed on in the centre of the airframe. Pax including me and Jen file up each side before buckling in to our seats. The Chinook is airborne, so the second leg of our trip home had started. Bastion is as busy as ever, helicopters are coming in from every location. I get eyes on the Ugly call signs or Apaches; you never get to thank the pilots of these incredible machines, to us on the ground they are just another faceless call sign, albeit a very important one.

When we arrive at our Medical Headquarters we are met by Sgt Maj Justin Harris of 19 Squadron. He was pleased to see that we had gotten back in one piece although his sober greeting was the result of some bad news from our guys in Nad-e Ali. Patrol Base Argyll had been hit hard during last nights attack leaving three members of B Company with gunshot wounds, all of them had been shot inside the perimeter wall, thankfully no fatalities although the company would have to endure a further five days of madness and this news wasn't at all welcome; it served as fore warning of what was in store for 3 Commando Brigade taking over. The guys were being treated here in Bastion just a few hundred meters away. Dropping off our kit we head straight for the hospital. When 42 Commando replaced B Company of 5 Scots, the troop level increased.

The district would eventually need a force of over 1,500 soldiers to stabilise it. Operation Sond Chara (Red Dagger in Pashto) was an 18-day campaign with its aims and objectives centered around four Taliban strongholds near the town of Nad-e Ali. The operation was named after the commando insignia worn by members of 3 Commando Brigade Royal Marines. 1,500 British troops were involved, supported by Danish, Estonian and Afghan forces in the pre-Christmas offensive.

The offensive was aimed to make safe the area around the capital of Helmand, Lashkar Gah. After an ever increasing amount of insurgent attacks the Taliban had planned to overrun the provincial capital with a 300-strong force. The defence of Nad-e Ali cost five British soldiers, including an Australian serving with British forces, their lives. This was over a short period of three months. God knows how many Afghan soldiers have been killed.

The bloody battles fought by the Commandos put into perspective what the men of B Company (5 Scots) achieved. They had held Nad-e Ali against all odds, somehow managing to subdue a very determined enemy. I was proud to have been a part of it, enjoying both the worst and best times of my life there. Bastion was a hive of activity the RIP or Relief In Place was in full motion.

3 Commando Brigade were anxiously waiting to get stuck into their tour of Helmand. Our battle worn Brigade had started its draw-down, we would grieve for our fallen when we got home. Walking through the tented camp on my way to the coffee shop I see my old friend Phil Train, he had been based in the notorious district of Sangin, it was a relief to see that he was okay and like me he had lost a fair amount of weight. We chat about our experiences, albeit in different areas. He laughs when I tell him about my escapades in Nad-e Ali.

Time was pressing on. I leave Phil and head over to our own Quartermaster Department to hand in my ammunition. Dreading another epic failure to move as quickly as I would like, I gut my magazines and have each clip of ammo ready for inspection. That way the jobsworth can't fuck up the count. Ten rounds per clip, how hard could that be? It always seems to take longer to get out of country than it does to get in. Flights are always delayed; kit is usually missing and then found in the same place that you put it.

Our next move was boarding the Hercules transport plane to KAF or Kandahar Air Force Base. Since the US Marines and elements of the 10th Mountain Division came here in late November 2001, when coalition forces entered Afghanistan it has grown.

The base has expanded into a small city housing over 30,000 multinational troops. The population consumes nearly 37,000 gallons (140,000 litres) of water and 50,000 meals a day at six different military restaurants. Though seen as far from the frontline of Helmand, Kandahar suffers from regular rocket attacks which have resulted in numerous KIA and casualties. Step outside the wire and you are straight into the middle of the official home of the Taliban.

We would spend one night at the airbase. The US certainly know how to go to war, they often bear the brunt of bad publicity about their overzealous use of force but the truth is they give more to these causes than anyone else in the world. We would not have functioned in Helmand if it weren't for the use of American assets. Our politicians are writing cheques that we as a well trained military cannot possibly cash. Our morning departure is here in a flash, after a quick shower I indulge in an all-American breakfast. The DEFAC is the US version of our cookhouse, its purpose is to feed soldiers and that's where the similarity ends. This place was something else, seven hot plates serving a variety of food to cater for the many different nations based here. There are fridges full of every type of drink that you can think of, the latest coffee machines and a quick order bar if you fancied something fresh.

They had absolutely everything you could think of. After gorging myself on pancakes and syrup I roll out of the DEFAC. I was bouncing from the sugar rush along to the departures area of the airfield. As my kit is loaded onto the back of one of many four ton trucks and I am instantly reminded of an incident that very nearly had me sent home early during the initial weeks of my tour.I along with elements of B Company were sent on a 48 hr Deliberate Op to the area of Babaji, north of Lashkar Gah. It was a district renowned for poppy cultivation. The Poppy Eradication Force (PEF) had been operating in the area for some time. Sustaining multiple casualties they were in imminent danger of being overrun. The PEF were all over the place, they were getting hit at every opportunity. We were sent to provide a screen for them to move safely out of the area. I was excited at the thought of getting amongst it so soon into the tour.

We were moving by helicopter to Bastion, there we would meet up with the Viking crews manned by Royal Marines and use their tracked vehicles to manoeuvre out to Babaji. After flying in from Lash we moved straight onto the back of four ton trucks, climbing up over the tail gate proved difficult with the weight of all my kit. Driving along, I sat chatting to the soldier next to me when suddenly I had the shock of my life.

Out of nowhere the side of the vehicle that we were sitting against came away. I was thrown out, along with another passenger crashing to the road. I landed on my back. Winded from my body armour and heavy kit I could barely breathe. Thinking that I had done something serious and unable to move I started to panic. Jen and Sean had thankfully deployed out with me, they were shocked at the sight of me stranded like an upside down turtle in the middle of the road.

All I kept thinking about was that this was the way that my tour would end. I had spent months doing hideous infantry courses, getting beasted on all the shite training areas that the British military had to offer, only managing to escape Otterburn. All that effort to end up falling out the side of a moving four tonner. An ambulance arrived at the scene; I managed to stand not realizing that I was going into shock. Medics always make the worst patients, I was still struggling to breathe, my body felt like I had been hit by a train. Surprisingly I had no serious injuries; this was the story of my life. I was always hurting myself enough to make tasks extremely uncomfortable but never enough to stop me doing the task. I spent the whole mission in agony. The right side of my body was purple and black with bruising, I was a mess. To make matters worse this was my first encounter with my Company Commander.

It was not the initial impression that I had hoped to give Major Harry Clark. Crammed in the back of a Viking for the entire time, this had to be my lowest point of the tour. At that stage I was just two weeks into my tour. As with everything though one positive did come out of the Op to Babaji and that was the birth of my multi-purpose yellow sharps container. Every cloud has a silver lining I suppose.

Our lives are now in the hands of the RAF, a movements Sgt stands on a box in the middle of the tent shouting 'Sir's, Ma'am's, ladies and gents' the same old shite that you hear every time you deploy anywhere, I wondered if he was taught that line during his arse-clown training. 'There has been a change of plan; your flight has been delayed!' the well versed Sgt reveals.

Shit I thought, we can do without delays. I took a gulp of water as my brain started to think exactly when we would get to Cyprus. 'Coffee and Tea are available in the dining facility; no weapons allowed I'm afraid', he adds. One of the guys says that bags must be checked in at 4 pm, amazing considering that out flight is at 2 am, still this is the RAF. With time on our hands we opt to take a wander around Kandahar (KAF) We head straight for the PX; it's a sort of supermarket for the US military selling everything from watches to televisions, clothing and perfume.

When I first came to KAF in 2006 the base was well established, by 2008 the place was unbelievable, a hive of military activity. It now had an area of half a square mile of covered walkways boasting some interesting shops. A German military kiosk sells souvenir burqas, there is a Thai restaurant, a steak house and all of this against a backdrop of Black Hawks, C-130's, and Apaches. It's hard to explain but something didn't seem right, with all this luxury you were in danger of relaxing too much. The mindset of people cutting about on mountain bikes appeared wrong, and was very different to the mind set of those in Helmand. We walked around like tourists, drinking our Frappes in silence. I knew that we were all going through the same process, everyone returning from Helmand probably felt the same, maybe that's what all the delays are designed for, it allows you to take gradual steps before hitting the streets of the UK.

As the sun began to disappear it was again time to indulge in the culinary delights of the DEFAC. Our journey to the terminal was interrupted by loud sirens, indicating that the base was under attack. Indirect Fire was becoming very accurate in KAF; and I wouldn't be taking any chances so close to getting home. Helmet and body armour on and straight into cover we go. Once the all clear is given we continue on with our journey to the terminal.

As we line up to check in I amuse myself by studying the cabinet of weapons and illegal items that people have tried to take home. A grenade, bits of rifles, 7.62 mm rounds, swords and pistols. The words 'full retard' were back in my head again thinking about the type of clown that would try and take shit through the security checks. I can imagine the scene as the idiot tries to explain to the RAF police, who search our kit. 'Well uh I decided that this RPG would look good in my room back in the Sgt's Mess!' I pictured the scene in my head.

Next we get our passports and British Army ID's checked by RAF flight staff; we enjoy a further two hour delay due to a snag in the 'missile decoy' system. Past caring I am happy to be sitting on a plane that was homeward bound. Putting my body armor and helmet on I grumble and wonder what possible benefit I am going to get by placing this cumbersome outdated kit on. If this plane goes down or crashes with a full tank of fuel then there would be a strong possibility that my little Mark 6 Alpha helmet was probably not going to make it.

We land in Cyprus under the cover of darkness and pile onto a long line of coaches to be moved to the camp that will house us for the evening. Tunnel beach awaits us. We can swim, drink beer and eat more decent food.

Lying out in the sun looking out to sea was as peaceful as it got, like all military fun tasks though we had to partake in the military swim test first for safety.

A couple of minutes treading water before a distance swim, to ensure that you weren't going to drown whilst playing on the many available inflatables. The British military is the best in the world at draining the fun aspect from most sporting activities.

The two beers I have go straight to my head which leave me feeling tired, drunk and I barely get through the night time entertainment of the two comedians. Decompression if anything is a good time to catch up with friends. Boarding the plane for the final leg home I get comfortable ensuring that my iPod is fully charged. This was the longest leg of the journey so I am grateful for the window seat, this way I won't wake up dribbling all over a complete stranger.

Landing at Stansted Airport was painless, close to Colchester it made for an easy coach ride if we caught the traffic right. For once baggage collection goes smoothly it might have had something to do with the fact that the RAF weren't controlling it. Passengers for Colchester are ushered onto waiting coaches. For the first time in a long time I ponder on nothing, I have six months left of military service and I am excited about the prospect of something new.

As a commander I became more relaxed than ever, I had learnt a great deal in Nad-e Ali and was eager to pass it on before I closed the book on my military life.

I was sent with a team of medics to Germany to help prepare the medical unit deploying to Helmand. This only reaffirmed my notion to leave. The medics under instruction did not take kindly to the advice that was on offer, when I left Germany I realised that my unit differed from all others.

On all levels 16 Close Support Medical Regiment is far more advanced when it comes to training its medics. 16 Close Support Medical Regiment, RAMC was formed in 1999 from the amalgamation of 19 Airmobile Field Ambulance and 23 Parachute Field Ambulance. Between the two units they had been involved in every major operation since World War Two.

After the union of both units the Regiment had seen action in Sierra Leone, Bosnia and Kosovo Iraq and most recently southern Afghanistan. The Regiment provides dedicated medical support to 16 Air Assault Brigade and will be called upon to support the complete spectrum of air assault operations. This will include airmobile, helicopter and parachute deployments. A percentage of the regiment must be parachute trained to support the on-call readiness force , known as the ABTF (Airborne Task Force).

Two regular Air Assault Medical Surgical Groups, each provide Role 2 medical support and resuscitative surgery. In addition to the regular squadrons, the Regiment is bolstered by a Territorial Army squadron. Called 144 Parachute Medical Squadron it is a permanent part of the Regiment, and is based on London, Cardiff, Glasgow and Nottingham. The TA squadron is fully integrated within the Regiment and members deploy regularly on operations and exercises in support of the Brigade.

The majority of the professionals and skills of the Army Medical Services can be found within the Regiment. 16 Brigade had been fortunate enough to be staffed with some of the best Physicians that the Military had to offer, most going on to support Special Forces. Combat Medics posted in the Brigade were highly motivated. The will to succeed and be the very best at what we do was echoed throughout the ranks. My success now is much to do with time served in this unit.

The thought of someday leaving the Brigade had solidified my decision to leave the service. Unlike the infantry, medics can be posted every three years and I didn't embrace the option of being posted anywhere else.

CHAPTER TEN

Saying Goodbye

Only by the grace of God were I and so many others allowed to return home physically unscathed. Others weren't so lucky. Which brings me to the significance of today. It's the 30th June 2009 and my last day of military service. A group of us had gathered in Yates Wine Bar on North Hill in Colchester.

'To Phil'. Glasses are raised clinking together and the shout of 'Cheers' sounds across the bar. The carpet beneath my feet is sticky. It's early in the morning and ordinarily not the time to be drinking Jack Daniels and Coke, but today is different and the two double shots go down easy, I am anxious to sink a couple more before we leave. The wine bar is close to the Garrison church and the only place that's serving this early unless you want a cup of tea that is. The barmaid looks at our group through inquisitive eyes but as our group become louder she disappears off through the 'Staff Only' door. I take a chance to quickly dash upstairs to the toilet, through fear of getting caught short in a half hour or so. On my return my hand is met by yet another shot of Jack and Coke.

'Ready? Dave taps my shoulder as we make our way out onto the main street. Feeling a little light headed I reach for the spearmints in my bag. We walk the short distance down the hill towards St Peters, the Garrison church, only stopping to say hello to other friends that had gathered outside. The mood is light and the sound of laughter makes the situation a bit weird. The church feels cold, despite the bright sunshine outside, it dates back to 1086 and can accommodate more than 700 people.

Every space will be full today. Taking my seat I see the familiar faces of friends sitting in the pews to my left. A flash of guilt comes over me for not having kept in touch. Paratroopers start to fill the rows in front, their head-dress held in their hands. The deep maroon colour of their berets stands out when set to the back drop of the dark wood shelving that houses the hymn sheets. A quiet hum of conversation fills the church as the soldiers chat quietly to one another. Several officers arrive wearing their formal No 2's or Service Dress. The ushers show them to their seats at the front of the church close to Phil's family. The Brigade Commander arrives and takes his place alongside other officers from Brigade headquarters. Starting to feel the effects of the Jack Daniels and Coke it seemed my trip to the toilet was not all that I hoped it would be.

For a moment drifting off wondering what today means, I feel angry that this was to be the way that it had ended for my good friend Sgt Philip Train. Phil was a Paratrooper who served with 2nd Battalion The Parachute Regiment. Like me he was born in Plymouth where his mother, Phyllis, and brothers Jason and David still live. He was a quiet man with silver grey hair and piercing blue eyes that showed his determination, confidence and ease with himself.

When we met I knew he had an air of something different about him. For a start his kit and equipment always looked better than others. He didn't have an endless stream of pouches and his attention to detail was borderline on obsessive. He always said that if he didn't need to have it then he didn't carry it. Phil was attached to the Army training Depot in Bassingbourn from 2 Para. We had both been selected for a tour of duty as recruit instructors albeit from very different backgrounds. He was the very best in our training company and he gave me what I had so often longed for in the past; someone to learn from. For me the Army had always lacked female role models this had left me learning my craft from the blokes. It always appeared to me that most women serving back then didn't know how to pitch. They either tried too hard and became overbearingly butch or didn't try hard enough.

Then they were viewed as weak in character. I soon learned though that a fair few of the blokes didn't get it either. Learning from Phil would one day save my life. Many of my friends ask what it's like being a woman in the military. I believe it's all about balance and sometimes it's easy to get the balance wrong. It took me a long time to realise that different situations call for different faces.

I had been on every level, too much, too little and then I managed to get the balance right. It hadn't been easy and I credit my achievements with being brought up properly, albeit in a less fortunate area. This had given me the drive and determination to succeed. I copied Phil, and was amazed at how much easier life became when I learned how to soldier from a soldier. My manner became more assertive and I started to look at things differently, medicine was my forte and the area that I had become an expert in but equally important was knowing how to employ good medicine in a tactically unstable environment. Phil's leadership had set an important example to the young paratroopers deployed with him in Helmand during the summer tour of 2008. His unit suffered heavy losses as fighting intensified. I spent many hours exchanging war stories with Phil when we passed through Camp Bastion on our way home from the fighting.

We had chatted at length at the coffee shop over pizza. The worst thing about today was dealing with the fact that Phil had survived the notorious Sangin Valley of Helmand only to be killed in a motor bike crash. It just seemed so pointless and such a waste. In my eyes this warrior should, if he had to, have died on the battlefield.

Men like him should die as a grandfather telling war stories or die in action. That was the type of man that Phil was. The sound of the church organ interrupts my private thoughts and as my eyes are drawn to my left I see six paratroopers slowly marching as they bear Phil's coffin to the front of the church. Scotty and Des are amongst the pallbearers, the pain of losing one of their own etched on their faces. As they made their way forward all heads turn to look at the coffin and if they were thinking the same as me they must have seen images of Phil flash through their minds.

Phil's young wife Stacy stood silently, her head held high. Her dignified manner was a credit to the husband that she is saying goodbye to. She could see how much her husband was thought of and I hoped that she was able to draw strength and some degree of comfort from it. Phil's coffin was lowered onto its support. Several people spoke about Phil, each describing his honour and bravery. Then a simple statement was read, I don't recall who said it, but I remember smiling at the words.

'He was a good bloke' echoed around the church walls, it was more than a battle honour or an over thought speech. That was it, Phil was a good bloke and that's how he should be remembered. I had an overwhelming sense of pride as the ceremony came to a close.

The service then moved on to Colchester Cemetery. It was a short drive away, the traffic was busy and local people stood and watched Phil's coffin being driven through the streets. Colchester is a garrison town, its small population are extremely supportive of what they regard as their paratroopers. As we drive through the gates of the cemetery the sky is bright and the grounds are peaceful. We make our way into the crematorium and Phil's coffin is again carried by his men into the small room. Suddenly without warning a song starts to play and the words are louder than I expect. The lump in my throat no longer holds me together. Normally words from songs wouldn't really affect me but this was different. All the pomp and ceremony offered no comfort. Outside, soldiers from 2 Para fire a salute to Phil and the volley of rifle fire is deafening. Trying hard to compose myself I fumble in my bag realising that I don't have any tissues. What an idiot I thought, wiping my face on my jacket sleeve like a four year old. Of all my time serving as a soldier I prided myself on keeping it together.

I was a combat medic who was used to dealing with the less glamorous side of life, although when it's your friend and not just a picture on the news it is different. Looking at Phil's wife Stacy I wonder how she would cope, how would she even start to rebuild a life without him. As soldiers we come to expect that the worst could happen, but I don't believe that we truly understand the void that we leave behind. Stacy is one of many parents, young wives and new mothers having to rebuild their lives alone.

In time I am sure and hope that Stacy will find her way. I had never really thanked Phil for all that he had done for me. I had seen him a few days prior to the accident and we joked about him hosting the next barbeque. Never in a million years did I think that would never see him again. Putting much of what I had achieved personally as a soldier down to the time spent learning from him when we were posted as instructors.

Our group headed back to 2 Para Sergeants' Mess where Phil's friends and family had gathered. I had been based here for the last three years at Merville Barracks in Colchester, Essex, home to many units which form the Brigade. I had made lifelong friends here and had also deployed on two tours of Afghanistan. I was leaving the military to start a new life in the world of Private Security.

In Helmand, I became frustrated at the lack of resources and manpower which in my opinion, in 2006 left us exposed. In 2008, we lacked helicopters and instead were forced to drive around in lightly armoured vehicles on roads that the Taliban had littered with their crude but destructive road side bombs. Our government had an almost naive military appreciation that we, Task Force Helmand, controlled the battle space. In reality the insurgents had the tactical advantage and every soldier in Helmand knew that. Back in 2006, I recall the then Defence Secretary John Reid saying that he hoped not a single round would be fired on that tour.

Clearly he had been reading the wrong reports. It was hugely kinetic and intense fire-fights with insurgents were a daily occurrence. The first Brigade into Helmand, led by Brigadier Ed Butler, faced significant challenges. But by the end of the tour it was clear that the Brigade's main fighting force, 3 Para, had, under the command of Lt Col Stuart Tootal delivered a significant measure of 'tactical success' with very few resources. Despite the fact that the British took heavy casualties, they overcame almost all engagements with overwhelming force. The insurgents clearly identified that they could not fight and win in any face to face contacts. Attacks by the Taliban on UK forces had significantly reduced.

This may have been because they had ended their 'fighting season' but intelligence indicated that the enemy had taken a severe beating and their manpower had been seriously depleted. In a statement, Brigadier Butler's spokesman at the time, Lt Col David Reynolds, told the media : "There is evidence that the Taliban's tactical capability to mount large attacks on the battlefield, has been seriously degraded. But they remain a significant threat and the use of improvised explosive devices is a major concern".

By late 2006 it was clear that the insurgents had changed their tactics with more attention being given to the roadside bomb. They opted for smaller operations in which they would plant the IEDs and the volume of attacks soared.

When 3 Commando Brigade took over the reins of Helmand Province in October of 2006, many soldiers and senior officers had hoped that the overwhelming political aim would be to support the military with additional force. In military jargon it is called 'reinforcing success' – in simple terms putting more resources into the battle to deny the enemy the chance to regroup or re organise any form of resurgence. But despite requests from Brigadier Butler, which he has spoken about publicly, to deploy more troops and resources, they did not arrive.

The failure to reinforce that success quickly with more helicopters, more troops and better equipment led to an insurgency that became stronger than we would ever care to admit. The UK government failed to send more helicopters and only marginally increased the level of troops. We sent nearly 40,000 into Iraq, yet could only muster less than 3,500 for Afghanistan 2006. This number did rise to 10,000, but it was nothing like the figure that many suggested was really required.

In 2010, the Americans deployed more than 25,000 troops to Helmand, lifting the Coalition manpower level to more than 35,000, with the UK contribution at around 10,000. History may later suggest that this was the number that we had needed when we first entered southern Afghanistan. Road moves were our biggest danger especially as there was no national curfew imposed.

This alone gave the insurgents the cover of night to plant bombs. The lack of additional air assets gave us little chance of reinforcing any success. Helicopters provide commanders with speed and surprise. They are essential in dominating an enemy, especially in areas of difficult terrain such as southern Afghanistan. Our initial choice of armoured vehicles provided limited protection against IEDs or Rocket Propelled Grenades (RPGs).

Our mechanics added metal plates to vehicles to give more protection, but while this worked the weight reduced their capability and speed. It also put huge strain on gearboxes. But even with the best armour, across open desert the tracks of our vehicles cut a path through the sand which created a huge sand cloud and signalled to everyone, Taliban included, that we were in the area. No surprise and no speed.

The Soviets suffered catastrophic losses during their invasion of Afghanistan in 1979. They poured armoured vehicles into the country and the tactic failed. The then enemy, the Mujahadeen, simply laid mines and roadside bombs and mounted attack after attack on Soviet vehicles, killing thousands of Rusian soldiers.

From 2007 and into 2008 the UK seemed to adopt the same policy of using large numbers of armoured vehicles and the numbers of deaths from Improvised Explosive Devices (IEDs) soared. Had we not learned these lessons? The fighting man on the ground had been let down not by our commanders, but by politicians who failed to understand the problems the military faced and failed to respond quickly to requests for more fighting men and equipment. Our officers are second to none. For me as a medic the resources or rather lack of them, at the makeshift hospital in Bastion during the summer of 2006 is a case in point.

We had a limited capability to deal with serious wounds and in particular head injuries, forcing us to fly men to Kandahar to be treated by the Canadians. The sole reason that the Brigade fared so well medically at that time is much to do with the willingness and foresight of all hospital staff and support to adapt and overcome any shortfalls. Young doctors and surgeons pioneered treatments that saved both life and limb that ordinarily would have been lost. But it wasn't just general equipment and medical care, our surveillance support in the form of the Nimrod was very old. Sadly in 2006, we lost 14 personnel when an RAF Nimrod crashed near Kandahar. Our lack of capability to rescue our own soldiers from extreme incidents was further highlighted when a patrol became trapped in an un-marked legacy minefield. A legacy minefield is one which has been left behind by previous conflicts. After a catalogue of disastrous events, four severely injured men including my good friend Stu Pearson, had to lie in that minefield for an unacceptable length of time. This should not have been allowed to happen.

I recall returning to Kandahar from my mid-tour leave at the time of the incident. It was in the morning when I heard the news about Stu. I was desperate to get back to the hospital at Bastion so I could see him and make sure that he was okay.

The following day I booked in at the air-head and boarded an RAF Hercules for the short 40 minute journey to Bastion. As the flight touched down on the airstrip, I couldn't wait to get off. Hurrying from the transport I quickly dropped my kit off in the tented accommodation close to the hospital. Heading straight for the high dependency unit I asked one of the nurses where I could find Stu.

Nothing prepared me for the sight of him lying there. Walking through the canvas doors of the ward in Camp Bastion was one of the most emotionally charged moments of my life, feeling unsteady on my feet I couldn't control myself, I looked at Stu and mumbled 'You alright?' Unable to keep it together I started to cry as Stu looked up at me. There are moments in life when you need to be strong and resolute and there are times when you just can't control it. I think the tears came through sheer relief more than anything else, I was just glad that Stu was still alive. His eyes were glazed and watery, high on medication he knew that he was in a bad way. He had already had one leg amputated and was in danger of losing the second. Lying in the next bed was Cpl Stu Hale, also missing a leg, next to him another amputee Andrew Barlow. The four others injured that day were on the general ward on the other side of the tented hospital corridor.

Another good friend, Cpl Paul 'Tug' Hartley, Royal Army Medical Corp (RAMC) was also wounded. Luckily though he had avoided loss of limb. I left the room to compose myself. I was no help to Stu in this state. I felt a bit pathetic I couldn't do anything to help him.

Wiping my face I took a few deep breaths and went back in, struggling to find the right words I waffled on about my leave and other nonsense. What are you supposed to say in these circumstances? I wanted to hug him and tell him that everything was going to be okay. I held his hand as he was covered from head to toe in tubes and dressings. I didn't like the fact that he was the only one still awake, the others all looked so peaceful and yet Stu had to sit and contemplate all that had happened.

He kept asking me about his other leg and if he was going to lose it. This gave me a much needed purpose, so I set about getting answers from surgeons about his chances. The initial response wasn't great. Doctors were doing all that they could to save the second limb but the damage was severe. I was advised that the chances of saving the second leg were 50/50. The truth was it would be down to the healing post surgery. His condition was out of my control but something made me want to stay. Holding Stu's hand until his evacuation, I had to be sure that he didn't die.

By some miracle and the skill of our military surgeons and recovery nurses, Stu's second leg was saved.

Sitting by Stu I was very angry. Why weren't we better equipped to deal with this type of incident? Our heaviest helicopter was sent as the rescue helicopter, but its heavy downdraft prevented it from picking up soldiers. The Chinook could have been to blame for setting off the mine that killed Cpl Mark Wright who lay trapped in the minefield and died from his injuries. We had no capability to be able to deal with this hideous event.

We had no Combat Search and Rescue (CSAR) helicopter to winch the injured soldiers to safety. Our commanders were left with no choice but to do what soldiers always do and get on with the job and deal with the incident with the equipment that was available. But with no smaller aircraft in our own fleet it was left to the Americans who deployed two Black Hawks to carry out the rescue of our stricken soldiers. The aircraft flew to the scene from Kandahar some 40 minutes away. Our system or lack of it had failed our men. The incident left Cpl Stu Pearson (3 Para) , LCpl Stu Hale (3 Para) Andy Barlow (RRF) with lower limb amputations. Cpl Mark Wright was posthumously awarded the George Cross for his outstanding bravery and leadership during the incident.

Stu was decorated with the Queen's Gallantry Medal. Andy Barlow and Paul Hartley were both awarded the George Medal.All members of the patrol told how Mark wouldn't let them fall asleep during their four hour wait for rescue, this alone would have much to do with the fact that any of them survived at all. That patrol on that day would never have gone near the minefield had they been given an up to date map of the area. My decision to leave the Army was easy. Stu's experience left me doubtful that I could endure much more of the bullshit coming out of the mouths of politicians who were involved in decision making at the top.

When Brigadiers and commanding officers destined for great things start resigning, that says to me that things aren't as they should be. I never thought that I would muster the courage to move on but my intuition told me that it was time to go. The Army had helped shape the person that I had become. Having experienced so much during the 11 years that I had served, I wondered if any other career could satisfy me either mentally or physically.

The world of security contracting appealed to me most, the perfect bridge between leaving the forces and becoming a civilian again. Close protection (CP) or Protective Security Detail (PSD) seemed the most natural way to wean myself off my life as a soldier.

I set about using as much of my re-settlement time as possible to qualify in areas that were alien to me. Luckily, my trade as a combat medic was in great demand. I undertook training to become a close protection operative and secured employment with an American company operating out of Afghanistan. I had four weeks left in the UK to ponder on anything and everything. here I was preparing to make my way back to the country that was flooding the UK and Europe with its biggest export, Heroin. Using those weeks wisely I spent as much time with loved ones as possible. losing Phil had reminded me never to take friends or family for granted and I knew that seeing them again before Christmas was highly unlikely.

The day of my flight was drawing close, leaving my familiar world I left London's Heathrow, before making a short stop indulging in the luxury of Dubai. My transfer to Kabul was swift and before I knew it we were touching down at Kabul International Airport Afghanistan. As the hydraulic doors lifted the familiar smell hit me like a freight train and I almost dry-heaved. These weren't new smells I had been there before. It felt different without the instant respect that my British Army uniform gave me. Gone was the rank that I had earned in that uniform. There are Afghan National Police (ANP) providing security at Kabul airport.

They view me with suspicion and it is a look a that I do not appreciate. I'm travelling with two other medics, both former military. Taff is former Royal Navy and Robbie served as a combat medic with the Australian Army. Both are as apprehensive as me as we get in line to collect our baggage. I had created this situation for myself. Conscious of the fact that I don't have a weapon, my palms are sweaty.

Getting eyes on the Personal Security Detail that are moving me to my new home further highlights my now inner turmoil. Being given a ground brief and actions on contact and casualties by a dangerously overweight PSD lead was a world away from the start I had envisaged. Just to make matters worse I remember that I have no medical kit. Desperate to call my Regiment and tell them that a huge mistake had been made, I wondered what they would think if they knew that I was out here cutting about with no weapon to protect myself. We set off driving through the dusty roads of Kabul and all the signs of the destruction left behind after numerous roadside bombs were clear to see. I was amazed how the Afghan people continued to go about their daily business.

Scanning around looking for any dangers, I check windows for gunmen, alleyways for potential threats, motorcycles getting too close.

It's then that I realise that Kabul is very different from the Afghanistan that I was familiar with. Thinking about the last time that I moved by road here, suddenly overwhelmed by a feeling of regret i wondered if my decision would somehow bite me in the arse. I take a deep breath and mentally order myself to get a grip. I may have left the military but that was no excuse to start acting like a sack of shit.

I come up with a plan, identifying that there were plenty of weapons in the vehicle. I would probably be getting the overweight commander's M4 (American assault rifle) as there was no way on earth that he would be getting out of the vehicle quickly enough to be effective. It was still early September and the heat of Kabul was not as uncomfortable as the heat of Helmand Province in late July 2008. There was never any escape from it. Smiling about my concerns minutes before, I am reminded of Nad-e Ali and B Company 5 Scots.

Chapter Ten

Acknowledgements

After ground dumping my thoughts on paper over a period of six weeks in the late summer of 2009 I decided to send the raw text to my Mum and try to explain what I had been doing in Afghanistan when I was a serving soldier. It wasn't polished and only touched the surface of my time with B Company 5 Scots during their mission to hold Nade-ali. She wrote back and commented that my writing was developing into a good story and she enjoyed reading about the characters particularly young Duffy. I would never have contemplated writing this book if it hadn't been for her encouragement. I have enjoyed a lifetime of her wisdom 'you can stoop down and pick up anything Channy, try reaching for it'.

My family, without their continued support I would not be the person that I am today. Stacy Train. Relatives of Cpl Mark Wright (3 Para). Fallen Paratroopers Sgt Phil Train (2 Para), W02 Michael 'Mark' Williams (2 Para) and WO2 Colin 'Tom' Beckett (3 Para).

16 Close Support Medical Regiment has some of the finest medics that I have ever worked with, including Captain James Leonard, W01 Baz Cuthbert, W01 Justin Harris, W02 Colin Jess, and SSgt Guy Griffiths there are many more and far too many to mention.

My medical detachment in Nade-ali consisted of four very bright, reliable and loyal combat medics. Jen, Sean, Abbie and Gurung you are only ever as good as your team, I was extremely lucky to be your commander.

To all ground fighting support elements often taken for granted, The MERT, helicopter pilots and crews, RAF fighter pilots and crews, and all hospital staff at Camp Bastion.

Paratroopers Stu Pearson (3 Para) Sgt Paul Scott (2 Para) Sgt Mathew Desmond (2 Para) SSgt Lee Payne (2 Para) W02 Karl Mitchell (2 Para), Cpl Ryan Rogers (3 Para) and Cpl Paul 'Tug' Hartley GM (RAMC). LCpl Andy James.

Jeff and Bev at the Fox and Fiddler, for making life feel that bit special when we come home.

Michael Rainwater (former Captain US Marine) Theodore Davis (former US Army), Jodie Grenier (former US Marine), SSgt Stephanie Vella and SSgt Sarah Halford.

The men of B Company (5 Scots) and the soldiers of the Afghan National Army. Lt Col Nazim (ANA), Maj Clark, Capt Wood, Lt Barclay, 2Lt Du Boulay for their leadership. Davey and Monty for their loyalty and friendship and making a sometimes hopeless situation bearable.

WO2 Tony Mason (Royal Irish) and all members of the OMLT. The 'Throatcutter' callsign.

Glossary of Terms

81 -	81 mm mortar round
9-liner -	9 Line MEDEVAC request
AA -	Air Assault
A/C -	Aircraft
ABP -	Afghan Border Police
AC-130 -	Gunship adapted from a Hercules
ACM -	Anti Coalition Militia
AFG -	Afghans
AK-47 -	Assault rifle used by insurgents
ANA -	Afghan National Army
ANAP -	Afghan National Auxillery Police
ANBP -	Afghan National Border Police
ANP -	Afghan National Police
ANSF -	Afghan National Security Forces
AO -	Area of Operations
AQ -	Al Qaida
AUP -	Afghan Uniformed Police
Blue on Blue -	Friendly fire
BRF -	Brigade Reconnaissance Force
Brew -	Hot drink
BSN -	Camp Bastion
C/S -	Call sign
CAS -	Close air support

CAT C -	Category C patient - priority casualty
CAT B -	Category B patient - Serious but stable casualty
CAT A -	Category A patient - Superficial wounds 'walking wounded'
CF -	Coalition Forces
CIVCAS -	Civilian casualties
CMT -	Combat Medical Team
CO -	Commanding Officer
COY -	Company
CP -	Checkpoint
DC -	District Centre
DSHKA -	Russian-made heavy calibre machine gun
EOD -	Explosive Ordinance Disposal (bomb disposal)
evac -	Evacuation
FO -	Forward Observer
FOB -	Forward Operating Base
GIRoA -	Government of the Islamic Republic of Afghanistan
Herrick -	The operational name given to British forces in Afghanistan
IDF -	In-direct Fire
IED -	Improvised Explosive Device
IFAK -	Individual First Aid Kit
Illum -	Illumination mortar round fire to provide light
INFIL -	Infiltrate
INS -	Insurgents

INTSUM -	Intelligence Summary
IO -	Information Operations
ISAF -	International Security Assistance Force
KIA -	Killed in action
MOD -	Ministry of Defence
OIC -	Officer in Charge
Op -	Operation
OP -	Observation Post
PEF -	Poppy Eradication Force (Afghan Police)
PF -	Path Finders (16 Air Assault Brigade)
JTAC -	Joint Terminal Air Controller
KAF -	Kandahar Airfield
LEP -	Law Enforcement Professionals
LKG -	Lashkar-Gah
PKM -	Russian-made light machine gun
PRT -	Provincial Reconstruction Team
QRF -	Quick Response Force
RPG -	Russian-made rocket propelled grenade launcher
Scoff -	Food
Shura -	A meeting of tribal elders and Afghan leaders
TB -	Taliban
TTPs -	Tactics, techniques and procedures
UAV -	Unmanned Aerial Vehicle (drone)
UH-60 -	Black Hawk, a helicopter used by American forces
VCP -	Vehicle Check Point

w/d - Wheels down

w/u - Wheels up

WIA - Wounded in action

Index